Sally Meyer Wolf

M.T. Publishing Company, Inc.™

P.O. Box 6802, Evansville, Indiana 47719-6802
www.mtpublishing.com

Copyright © 2015 Indiana Bicentennial Commission
All rights reserved.

Library of Congress Control Number:
2015944762

ISBN:978-1-938730-66-5

Graphic Design by: Alena L. Kiefer
M.T. Publishing Company, Inc.™

Out of 1,800 books printed, this book is number
656 .

Printed in Indiana, United States of America.

Dedication

Indiana at 200: A Celebration of the Hoosier State is a patchwork quilt of images, prose and poetry commemorating our bicentennial. Incorporating a wide variety of Hoosier voices—individual, yet bound together by a common Hoosier heritage—this book reflects the thoughts of business and community leaders, artists, athletes, writers, farmers, religious leaders, children and poets. These voices, along with many of the more than 6,000 photos submitted by amateur and professional photographers throughout the state, present a picture of who we are as Hoosiers, as well as our dreams and aspirations. We hope you enjoy this commemoration of our shared experience.

~Becky Skillman and Lee Hamilton, Indiana Bicentennial Commission Co-chairs

Indiana Bicentennial Commission

Becky Skillman, Co-chair
Lee H. Hamilton, Co-chair
First Lady Karen Pence, Bicentennial
    Ambassador
Sarah Evans Barker, Judge
Charlie Brown
Dr. Howard Cohen
Stephen L. Ferguson
Anton H. George
P.E. MacAllister
James H. Madison
Michael S. Maurer
Mary McConnell
C. James McCormick
James W. Merritt Jr.
Ellen M. Rosenthal
Randall T. Shepard

Bicentennial Commission Staff

Perry T. Hammock, Executive Director
E. René Stanley
Valeri E. Beamer
Samuel L. Alderfer
Adrienne Smith
Ariana A. Smith
Rachel K. Beliles
Christopher T. Jensen (2011-2014)
Deborah Wezensky (2013-2014)

Edited by Lisa Hendrickson with Alicia Carlson and Tom Harton

The Indiana Bicentennial Commission extends its sincere thanks to the sponsors who have made publication of this book possible:

Underwriting Sponsor
Anton H. George
Indianapolis, Indiana

Presenting Sponsor
Steve and Connie Ferguson
Bloomington, Indiana

Thank you to our production partner, M.T. Publishing Company, Inc. of Evansville, Indiana, for underwriting the production of the book.

Denise Szocka, Indiana Department of Environmental Management

4

Essayists
Pete Buttigieg
Philip Gulley
Bob Hammel
Paul Helmke
David Lawther Johnson
Sen. Richard G. Lugar
Barbara Olenyik Morrow
Susan Neville
Sandy Eisenberg Sasso
Sharon Sorenson
Andrew B. Takami
Gene Tempel
John Thompson
Eunice Trotter
Mauri Williamson

Poets
William Buckley
Jared Carter
Mari Evans
George Kalamaras
Elizabeth Krajeck
Norbert Krapf
Orlando Menes
Christine Montross

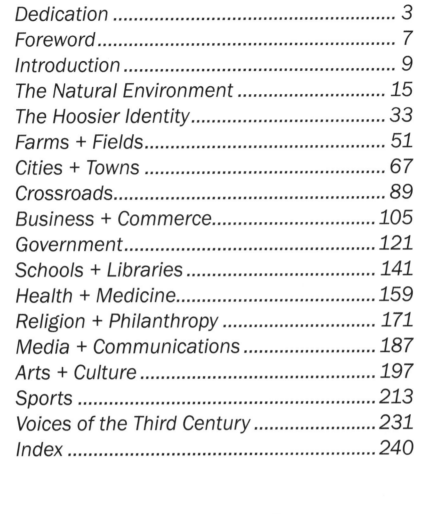

Table of Contents

Dust jacket/cover photo credits: Lesley Ackman, Sean Aikins, Felicia Batman, Beth El Zedeck Early Education, Steve Blackwell, Brad Brown, Richard Bryant, Andrea Curry, Downtown Indy, James Eickman, Mark A. Einselen, Robert E. Geary, Perry Hammock, Indianapolis International Airport, Jill Levenhagen, Freddie Kelvin, Marian University, Eddie Relick, Jim Rettker, Jennifer Zartman Romano, Thomas Semesky, René Stanley, Denise Szocka, Twila Usrey, Charlie Winstead

Paul Hadley of Mooresville, left, who designed Indiana's state flag, watches as Ralph E. Priest, a student at John Herron Art Institute in Indianapolis, applies gold leaf to the flag sometime around 1923. The Indiana General Assembly adopted the state flag in 1917. Hadley's design was selected in an Indiana centennial celebration contest.

Indiana Historical Bureau

Foreword

As we Hoosiers celebrate our state's bicentennial, let us take this moment to honor our proud heritage and imagine the bright and prosperous future that, together, we are building for tomorrow.

As we look back on 200 years of statehood, we bear witness to a history marked with challenges that earlier generations rose to overcome.

When Indiana was admitted to the Union on Dec. 11, 1816, we became the first state born in the aftermath of the War of 1812. Our forebears were builders and farmers—people of fortitude and courage, men and women who chose to brave harsh weather and hardship to build both their futures and a new state in an untamed land.

In those early days of statehood, a family with the last name Lincoln settled in southern Indiana. Years later, the son, Abraham Lincoln, would remember Indiana as "a wild region, with many bears and wild animals in the woods."

Our first state constitution was written under the shade of an elm tree in Corydon in 1816 mostly by ordinary citizens and frontiersmen. In writing our state's charter, early Hoosiers lit a beacon of civilization, hope and freedom in this state carved from the Northwest Territory.

One hundred years later, that fact would inspire the design of our state flag. Crafted during the state's 1916 centennial celebration, our flag displays a gold torch and 19 stars on a field of blue. A circle of 13 stars symbolizes the 13 original colonies. Five additional stars symbolize the next states admitted into the Union. And the large, single star located above the flame of the torch stands for Indiana—the 19th state.

Now another century has passed.

We Hoosiers still draw inspiration and strength from some of the same sources to which our ancestors turned—faith, music, art, poetry.

Today, though, we enjoy forms of technology, communications, transportation, education, industry, medicine, agriculture and commerce that our ancestors could scarcely have imagined.

By embracing change and innovation, we lead the nation in many sectors of society. Our successes reflect our best Hoosier values: the cordial manner of our citizens, our shared love of family and neighbors, our strong sense of patriotism and independence, our devotion to this land that is Indiana, and an abiding commitment to hard work and honesty. For Hoosiers, these elements define the word "home."

We hope for even greater things for our children, our grandchildren and generations to follow. Let us dedicate the fruits of our labors to them because, truly, their future is Indiana's future.

Among the best traditions of Hoosiers is a commitment to respect one another, work together and ultimately find ways to forge wise paths forward.

In that spirit, let's write the next great chapter of Indiana history.

~ Gov. Mike Pence

Perry Hammock, Indiana Bicentennial Commission
Gov. Mike Pence stands beside the city of Bedford's bicentennial-themed bus, one of more than 500 Indiana Bicentennial Legacy Projects.

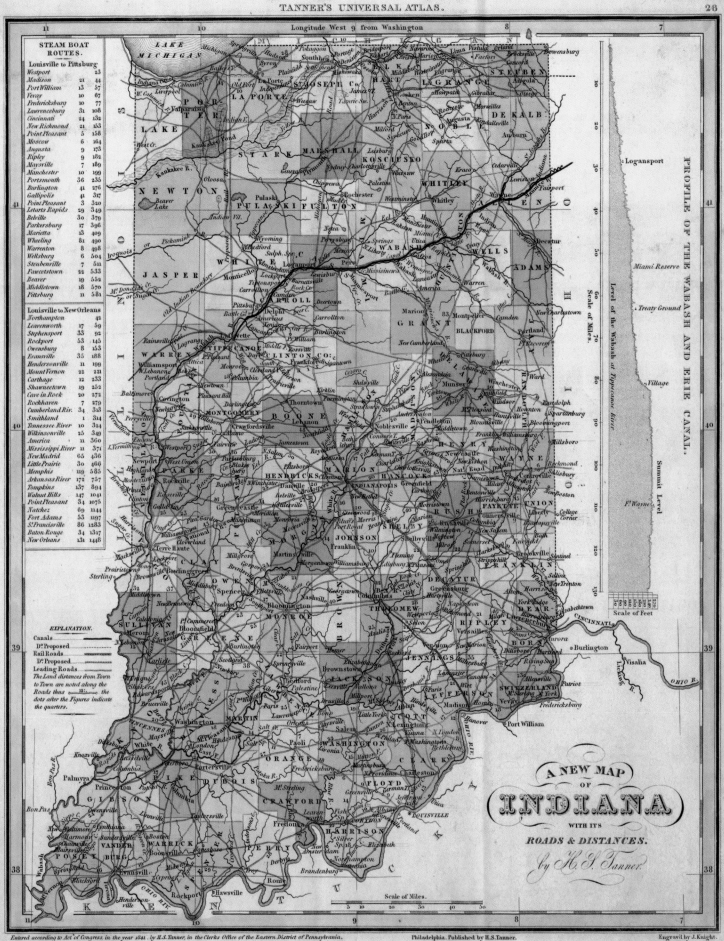

By Sen. Richard G. Lugar

We were off to a good start when the Congress of the United States passed the Northwest Ordinance in 1787 and created the Indiana Territory in 1800 as one of the Northwest Ordinance's two territories. President John Adams appointed William Henry Harrison, who was later to serve as president in 1841, as governor. Representative government was adopted by a citizen referendum in 1804, advancing Indiana to the second stage of territorial government.

Suffrage would include white males who owned property. Slavery was prohibited by the Northwest Ordinance but the struggle over its place continued until adoption of the Indiana Constitution in 1816. The Harrison Land law adopted by the U.S. Congress in 1800 provided for land to be purchased, with the minimum amount being 320 acres at $2 per acre. The minimum was reduced to 160 acres in 1804, with generous credit promises. After an economic depression, 80 acres at $1.25 an acre was the new standard, with all purchases to be in cash.

The Indiana General Assembly sought statehood in 1801 but did not succeed until a successful petition in 1815 and a state constitution was drafted at Corydon. Following the organization of a state government, the U.S. Congress granted statehood to Indiana on Dec. 11, 1816. In 1816, Indiana had only 15 counties. The census of 1800 found that the Indiana Territory had a population of only 5,641, but dynamic growth followed, with Indiana's population reaching nearly one million by 1850. In 1840, four-fifths of the population was in the southern half of the state. Native Americans, primarily located in northern Indiana, had moved to an area west of the Mississippi River following treaties negotiated by their leaders.

continued

Indiana map, 1841
Indiana Historical Society

The large population growth was driven by citizens of German, Irish, English and Polish heritage. A great many Hoosiers trace their lineage to these ethnic groups. In the mid-1980s as chairman of the U.S. Senate Committee on Foreign Relations, I was planning to visit with German leadership. Our U.S. ambassador to Germany, Arthur Burns, urged me to research my family tree and German heritage before I landed in Germany. It was good advice. The Lugar family's flow from Germany to Virginia, Virginia to rural Indiana, from rural northern Indiana to suburban central Indiana and then to Indianapolis was a typical family history over the last 200 years. Utilizing two centuries of the Lugar family tree, I went to Germany with proposals for German-American diplomatic and military unity, despite a dramatic family event at the beginning of my family's journey.

Specifically, my ancestor, Adam Lugar, came to America as a Hessian soldier. Fortunately, he deserted soon after arrival and fought with the American revolutionaries in several battles over the next 18 months. He was rewarded with a land grant in Salem County, Virginia, and became a successful farmer. One of his sons, George Lugar, moved to Grant County, Indiana, in 1838. He lived on a waterway that he named Lugar Creek and farmed land now included inside the boundaries of Marion, Indiana.

His grandson, Joseph Lugar Jr., who farmed 531 acres and served as a county commissioner, volunteered in May 1861 to preserve the Union and to halt the advance of the Confederacy. By the end of the Civil War, Indiana, the first western state to mobilize for the Union, had organized approximately 200,000 men. More than 25,000 Hoosier lives were lost and more than 50,000 Hoosiers were wounded. Only one battle, the Battle of Corydon, was fought in Indiana.

One of Joseph Lugar's sons, Riley Webster Lugar, my paternal grandfather, moved his family to Decatur Township of Marion County. He continued the family farming tradition and his oldest son, my father, Marvin L. Lugar, graduated from Valley Mills High School and proceeded to the Purdue University School of Agriculture and the Purdue basketball team coached by the legendary Piggy Lambert.

> *"I suggested that although the sport of basketball had been founded by James Naismith, Naismith declared that Indiana was surely the developer of school basketball."*

On another diplomatic assignment during my Foreign Relations Committee chairmanship, I was asked by President Ronald Reagan to lead a delegation to the Philippines to monitor a "snap" election called by President Ferdinand Marcos in 1986. During a subsequent visit, following the dramatic leadership turnover to Corazon Aquino, I turned on the television one night and in the company of distinguished Filipinos watched the movie "Hoosiers," inspired by the story of Milan High School winning the Indiana high school basketball tournament.

I suggested that although the sport of basketball had been founded by James Naismith, Naismith declared that Indiana was surely the developer of school basketball. My friends accepted this but wanted an explanation of the meaning of "Hoosiers." My answer was complex and focused on the passions and productivity of our state rather than on the etymology of the word. I pointed out that the first successful auto company, Haynes-Apperson, was in Kokomo, Indiana. The development of the Indianapolis Motor Speedway, with seating capacity of 257,325 and its 500-mile race, named "the greatest spectacle in racing," flowed out of Hoosier innovation. During World War II, in which the United States fought alongside the Philippines, 10 percent of Hoosiers joined the armed forces. Indiana ranked eighth among the 48 states in military arms production.

Following World War II, auto, steel and pharmaceuticals led industrial growth and Indiana cities grew substantially. Historically, strong agriculture traditions and expertise led to dramatically greater production on farms through development of better seeds, fertilizers, soil management and huge sophisticated machinery. In 1949 the Indiana General Assembly passed legislation desegregating Indiana schools— although this was not achieved finally until federal action occurred—and in 1961 Gov. Matthew Welsh signed into law the Indiana Civil Rights bill. All of these developments helped to define "Hoosiers" for my Filipino friends in the 1980s.

But as we celebrate the Indiana bicentennial, it has been apparent for several years that the next century of growth and vitality in Indiana will require many new bursts of imagination, innovation and new products, service and procedures, plus dramatically heightened interaction with countries all over the world.

In 2015, President Barack Obama visited Ivy Tech and while praising its 200,000 students proposed a policy of two years of no tuition for community college students, which might stimulate a substantial increase in higher-learning opportunities.

In 2014, a host of foreign ambassadors in the United States discussed in Bloomington our nation's participation in

World War I but also praised the expanding School of Global and International Studies at Indiana University, which offers instruction in almost 100 languages. Hoosier "millennials" have often stated that they yearn for independent and ambitious "anti-establishment thoughts and actions," which we should all pray result in new startup companies and new associations that produce jobs and significant research breakthroughs in new products and services.

In a world of continuing huge population growth, demand for Hoosier agriculture production will increase despite occasional tariff and trade barriers. Perhaps we can find new healthy food and energy products as we continue to increase yields on our farms. Our great pharmaceutical giants must continue to find new ways to reduce the suffering and extend the healthy lives of people worldwide. 2016, the year of Indiana's bicentennial, will surely be a year in which we take time to remember our history, our churches and schools, and the many ways we have strengthened hope and happiness.

2016 must also be a year in which we make an honest appraisal of the future of Indiana. Hoosiers who will celebrate Indiana's tricentennial must note and remember that in 2016, we established an upward trend line. As we celebrated 2016, we were planning, innovating, investing and encouraging each other as we sang "Back Home Again in Indiana."

Richard Lugar served as U.S. senator from Indiana from 1977-2013. He was mayor of Indianapolis from 1968-1975.

Sen. Richard Lugar at his Marion County farm

Courtney Eckstein

Indiana Population
1800: 5,641*
1810: 24,520
1820: 147,718
1840: 685,866
1850: 988,416
1880: 1,978,301
1910: 2,700,876
2010: 6,483,802
* Indiana Territory

Source: U.S. Census

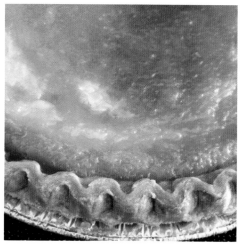

René Stanley, Indiana Bicentennial Commission

State Pie: Sugar Cream

Brad Brown

State Bird: Cardinal

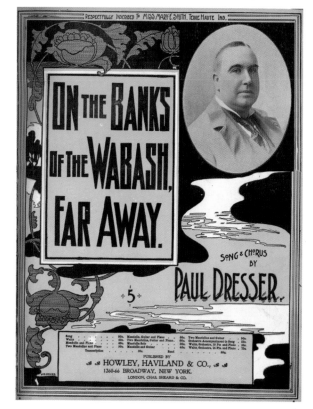

Vigo County Historical Society and Museum

Sharon Sorenson

State Tree: Tulip Tree

Felicia Batman

State Flower: Peony

"*On the Banks of the Wabash, Far Away*," written by Terre Haute native Paul Dresser and dedicated to 14-year-old Mary E. South of Terre Haute, whom Dresser had never met, is the state song of Indiana. First published in July 1897, the song was adopted as the official state song on March 14, 1913 by the Indiana General Assembly. The state song is the oldest of Indiana's state emblems, adopted four years before the flag.

On the Banks of the Wabash, Far Away
(Final stanza)

Oh, the moonlight's fair tonight along the Wabash,
From the fields there comes the breath of new mown hay.
Thro' the sycamores the candle lights are gleaming,
On the banks of the Wabash, far away.

Rona Schwarz

State River: Wabash River

Portrait of William Henry Harrison, first governor of the Indiana Territory, appointed in 1800 by President John Adams

The history of this 1874 cabin at the Cass County Historical Society tells much about the self-reliant, rugged pioneers who settled Indiana.

Indiana's first state Capitol building in Corydon was built in 1816, the year Indiana became a state. Corydon was named the territorial capital in 1813 and remained the Indiana state capital until 1825, when it moved to Indianapolis. Today the Harrison County landmark is part of the Corydon Capitol State Historic Site.

By Sharon Sorenson

Sandwiched between a great lake to the north and a great river to the south, Indiana boasts remarkable natural diversity. Landscape ranges from singing-sand dunes to prairie to wetlands to sprawling caves and the mysteriously disappearing-reappearing Lost River.

Prior to human settlement, 150-foot-tall hardwood forests blanketed 85 percent of the state, especially the hills of southern Indiana. As the Wisconsin Glacier retreated 15,000 years ago, it scraped level the upper two-thirds of the state, leaving the Indiana Dunes along Lake Michigan's shore. To the south, as the ice receded, glacial-melt floods carved river and ravine, creating the Knobstone Escarpment, its rocky namesake knobs rising 610 feet above the Ohio River.

Indiana's prehistoric roots also are revealed along the Falls of the Ohio, where 390-million-year-old fossil beds are among the largest naturally exposed Devonian fossil beds in the world. At the other end of the state, skeletal remains confirm a prehistoric vision of Hoosier lands that once served as home to thundering mastodons, saber-toothed tigers, giant beavers and a type of large elk.

Once the last glacier retreated, leaving behind its moraine, most of the state's watershed flowed into the Mississippi Basin, and of course still does. The Wabash River, even now the longest uninterrupted river east of the Rockies, drained the Hoosier state to the south. Northern portions of the state, however, were home to an unmatched wilderness. The nearly 1-million-acre Grand Kankakee Marsh, recognized then as the largest freshwater

continued

Spring Mill State Park, Lawrence County
Osterhage Photography

marsh in the Midwest, made the northwest section of the state impenetrable. Across the state to the northeast, the Great Black Swamp, penned by author Gene Stratton Porter as the "Limberlost," had a similar effect. In the middle, the tallgrass prairie undulated to its eastern end. Bison roamed the plains and woodlands and quenched their thirst on the banks of the Ohio, and the old buffalo trails gave our state's first settlers easy traverse.

But that was then; this is now.

After centuries of human habitation, Hoosier landscape has changed: wetlands drained, waterways straightened, prairies plowed, forests timbered, resources mined, limestone quarried and acres paved. As humans changed the habitat, so changed the wildlife. Some species, both flora and fauna, were extirpated. Ospreys, bald eagles and wild turkeys disappeared from the state; bison, elk, bobcat and American porcupine vanished. Today, more species decline as development and environmental deterioration raise the bar for wildlife survival.

> *"As early as 1916, a few farsighted folks initiated the call for conservation. Richard Lieber, father of the Indiana State Parks, professed the wisdom of setting aside protected lands. Progressive beyond his time, Lieber was considered, at least by some, to be this nation's most powerful spokesman for the conservation of natural resources."*

In short, when humans pull a single thread, the entire fabric begins to unravel.

Here's another way to think about Indiana's natural environment. Among the 400-plus birds roaming Indiana both permanently and seasonally, each demands a certain habitat in order to feed, drink, find shelter and reproduce. Now-lost forests once reverberated with the namesake calls of whippoorwills and flashed with the brilliant blue of abundant cerulean warblers. Today the whippoorwill's song rarely breaks the silence and cerulean warblers mostly fail to show. Disappearing grasslands once hosted the music of eastern meadowlarks and Henslow's sparrows; today their songs only infrequently join an overall quieter chorus. Fence rows and forest edges, today cleared and tidy, once protected northern bobwhites whistling their names; today they cling to survival in remote or restored patches of cover. I remember all these birds from my childhood, seeing them, hearing them, knowing them. Now, I miss them. But here's the extension of the missing birds: Other wildlife follows the avian pattern, their absences pointing to the health of the environment and serving as the canary in the coal mine. Today, the canary grows sick; we must pay attention.

As early as 1916, a few farsighted folks initiated the call for conservation. Richard Lieber, father of the Indiana State Parks, professed the wisdom of setting aside protected lands. Progressive beyond his time, Lieber was considered, at least by some, to be this nation's most powerful spokesman for the conservation of natural resources. Beginning with McCormick's Creek and Turkey Run in 1916 in celebration of Indiana's first 100 years, Lieber brought about during his lifetime the establishment of 10 state parks and five state memorials. Our most recent, O'Bannon Woods State Park in Harrison County, joined the protected lands in 2005; and the 26,000 acres of Harrison-Crawford State Forest surrounding O'Bannon and the famed Wyandotte Caves is the largest in Indiana. Last year, almost 17 million visitors found relaxation at our 34 Hoosier state parks and reservoirs. Beyond Lieber's state-protected lands, five Hoosier protected areas today carry national designations: Hoosier National Forest (Indiana's largest protected area); Indiana Dunes National Lakeshore; and Muscatatuck, Big Oaks and Patoka National Wildlife Refuges.

How do we fare now? Recent surveys show Hoosier forests blanket 4.5 million acres, more than double the 2 million acres 100 years ago. Still, it's a serious decline from the pre-settlement 23 million acres. Roughly 2,000 acres of original old-growth forest remain intact, most protected, some as National Natural Landmarks. Sadly, the only recognized wilderness area in the state is the 13,000-acre Charles C. Deam Wilderness Area, situated within the Hoosier National Forest, honoring the man who in 1909 became Indiana's first state forester.

While species of flora are now far less prolific than during Deam's lifetime when he discovered 25 new plant species, native wildflowers decorating Indiana lands still comprise a long list, including a surprising 43 species of orchids. The state's population of mammals, reptiles and amphibians is equally numerous. So is our list of insects, including a book-length array of lovely butterflies. But while we enjoy our native flora and fauna, we must come to grips with the fact that 390 plant species and 130 animals are now rare, threatened or endangered. Another 31 Hoosier native animals already are extinct.

And there's this: According to the Indiana Department of Natural Resources, "Approximately 4 percent of state lands are designated as conservation areas for native plants and animals, putting the state at No. 46 in the country in terms of conservation."

We can do better.

On the positive side, we have seen the return of breeding bald eagle in Hoosier lands. Osprey, peregrine falcon, wild turkey, white-tailed deer, bobcat and river otter have returned or been successfully reintroduced.

Public and private land trusts currently make some headway toward protecting precious parcels from further destruction. The development of the Bicentennial Nature Trust provides for permanent protection of Hoosier lands. Costly but effective, restoration efforts under the tutelage of The Nature Conservancy and others have returned at least a remnant of central tallgrass prairie to the more than 8,000-acre Kankakee Sands in northwest Indiana, where native plants now produce seas of

blossoms that lure birds' return. And after another herculean effort, 7,000 acres of wetlands were restored at Goose Pond Fish and Wildlife Area in Greene County, now recognized as one of the nation's finest. Astonishingly, birds like the king rail, undocumented in Indiana for more than 100 years, not only returned to the ancient wetlands but stayed and raised families.

The adage "Build it and they will come," brought to fruition by these efforts, has become the mantra—and model—for restoration nationwide. Given public desire, Indiana can lead the way for even broader conservation efforts, protecting and restoring the state's precious natural environment. As we celebrate our bicentennial, I fervently hope Hoosiers resolve to take that lead.

Naturalist Sharon Sorenson, Evansville, is the author of "Birds in the Yard Month by Month" and a columnist for the Evansville Courier & Press.

Matt Williams

The 390-million-year-old fossil beds at Falls of the Ohio State Park in Clark County. Falls of the Ohio National Wildlife Conservation Area, a series of rapids over the 386-million-year-old Devonian limestone rock shelves, marks the only navigational barrier on the Ohio River.

Jug Rock in Martin County holds the distinction of being the largest free-standing table-rock formation east of the Mississippi River. The sandstone pillar stands 60 feet tall and measures 20 feet wide.

Centuries ago, bison roamed Indiana's plains. In fact, the Buffalo Trace from Vincennes to New Albany was a major early trail for both buffalo and people. Today, bison are being reintroduced on a number of Hoosier farms. The bison pictured here have a home at Ouabache State Park in Bluffton.

Richard Lieber, first chairman of the Indiana State Parks Committee and the State Department of Conservation. He spearheaded the founding of McCormick's Creek and Turkey Run State Parks in 1916.

"We all hunger for the natural and spiritual, so let us seek it out in the undefiled wilderness—but, remember, you are not the heir, but the steward, of a great inheritance to be handed over to posterity."

~ Richard Lieber

Gene Stratton-Porter

Indiana State Library

INFact

Indiana's Footprint

36,185 square miles

Length: 275 miles

Breadth: 144 miles

253 square miles of water

Highest altitude: 1,257 feet, Wayne County

Lowest altitude: 320 feet, Posey County

Source: www.in.gov

Rebecca James

An American coot at Loblolly Marsh Wetland Preserve in Jay County. The preserve was originally part of the 13,000-acre Limberlost Swamp featured in famed Indiana author Gene Stratton-Porter's books. In 1997, the group Limberlost Swamp Remembered began restoring more than 428 acres of the land. In nearby Rome City is the Gene Stratton-Porter State Historic Site, where the author lived in her later years.

In Crawford County, visitors can view nature's underground architecture at Marengo Cave. Discovered by school children in 1883 and opened to the public shortly after, the cave's many formations brought it national recognition. It is one of only four show caves in the state.

Fall Creek Gorge in Warren County

Flooding has long been a fact of life along Indiana creeks and rivers. The Wabash River flood of 1913 inundated Lafayette and West Lafayette.

Every Hoosier is familiar with the wail of spring tornado sirens. The Palm Sunday tornado outbreak on April 11 and 12, 1965, was the deadliest ever recorded in state history. One hundred forty-five people were killed and 1,200 were injured in Indiana. This photo from Mishawaka recorded the storm's aftermath in St. Joseph County. The massive destruction prompted major reforms in weather-preparedness activities.

Flames consume the Upland Prairie Restoration Project in Grant County. A partnership between Taylor University's Earth and Environmental Sciences department and Avis Industrial Corporation, the prairie is burned each spring for maintenance.

Storm clouds roll in near Batesville.

Indiana Voices: Barbara Tibbets

Barbara Tibbets is a naturalist interpreter with the Indiana Department of Natural Resources.

"I've been camping and hiking at Turkey Run State Park for most of my life. As a child I never dreamed that I would one day get to work in such a beautiful and ecologically significant place. But in 1992 I was hired as the interpretive naturalist, and I've been a caretaker of the park ever since. It's a rewarding job, but one that comes with many challenges.

"Turkey Run is visited by three-quarters of a million people each year. With 11 hiking trails wandering through less than 2,400 acres, the park reels under the weight of human impacts. We try to educate our visitors through exhibits and programs that help them better understand the park's natural resources. We believe this can help reduce littering, tree carving and hiking off-trail into areas reserved for wildlife.

"We also work to remove non-native plants introduced by humans. These invaders crowd out our native plants, which reduces the numbers of both plants and animals that can live in the park. Humans have also worked to suppress natural fires that occasionally swept through Indiana forests, so we have brought fire back into the park in a controlled fashion. This helps to maintain fire-dependent plant communities like fens and oak-hickory forests.

"These days a large part of my time is spent recruiting, educating and training volunteers to help us accomplish these tasks. These natural areas are truly treasures, glimpses of this country before European settlement, places for refreshing the spirit, for getting away from the stresses of life for a little while. Saving our Indiana state parks for future generations is both an honor and our sacred duty."

Barbara Tibbets talks with visitors.

Deer were native to Indiana long before settlers arrived. This trio was found on the grounds of Conner Prairie in Hamilton County.

A bold raccoon reaches for a snack at Turkey Run State Park.

The Midwestern praying mantis spends its days foraging for insects to satisfy its large appetite.

Indiana Voices: Phil Meltzer

Retired Shelby County farmer Phil Meltzer and his family have ensured that Indiana's last remaining unprotected old-growth forest is preserved for future generations of Hoosiers. The Meltzers sold 60 acres of land that has been in their family for four generations to the Central Indiana Land Trust, Inc. (CILTI) for 50 percent of its appraised value. In 2016 Meltzer Woods will become a dedicated state nature preserve made possible with support from the Bicentennial Nature Trust, a project of the Indiana Bicentennial Commission. CILTI Executive Director Cliff Chapman says, "Meltzer Woods is a very special place. There aren't many places where Hoosiers can visit and see huge old trees that predate Indiana's statehood and, in this case, the birth of our nation."

Phil Meltzer next to an old-growth tree in Meltzer Woods

"My great-grandfather and his wife came over from Germany and bought a farm in 1857. It was a mile long and a quarter-mile wide. Most of Meltzer Woods is in that plot. A lot of people, when they came here from the old country, would protect the forests.

"After World War II, veneer prices got so high that my dad felt like he needed to sell some veneer oak and walnut, but he finally decided that he liked the trees better than the money. We weren't rich, but we had enough money to get by, and he loved the trees.

"I grew up liking the woods, and since the land had been in the family so long and my father liked it so well, I felt like I had to keep it too. There are some big oaks and walnuts, and a state champion black ash. It's got quite a few red-headed woodpeckers, a nest of hoot owls and squirrels, and a lot of old trees with holes in them.

"Right now my favorite spot in the woods is where the biggest tree, a Shumard oak, was blown over by the wind a couple of years ago. It had been a state champion for 25 years and was by far the biggest tree in the woods. It's on the ground now, and I think a sugar maple is going to take its place. It will lie right there and it will take years to go back into nature.

"We all feel good to know that Meltzer Woods will be preserved and that anybody can come and walk the trails. The way we think about it is, the greatest good is that which does the greatest good for the greatest number of people for the longest time."

INFact

Indiana's Remaining Old-Growth Forests

- Bendix Woods Nature Preserve: 27 acres, St. Joseph County
- Donaldson's Woods Nature Preserve: 67 acres within Spring Mill State Park, Lawrence County
- McClue Nature Preserve: 80 acres, Steuben County
- Pine Hills Nature Preserve: 470 acres within Shades State Park, Montgomery County
- Rocky Hollow-Falls Canyon Nature Preserve: 1,609 acres within Turkey Run State Park, Parke County
- Shrader-Weaver Nature Preserve: 108 acres, Fayette County
- Wesselman Woods Nature Preserve: 190 acres, Vanderburgh County

Source: Indiana Department of Natural Resources

A Martin County autumn landscape highlights Indiana's fall colors at their peak.

Hunting morel mushrooms in the springtime is a long-standing Hoosier pastime. The culinary treats shown above were discovered in Orange County.

An early spring fern unfurls in Union County's Horbeam Nature Preserve.

Colorful prairie flowers brighten this Kosciusko County field.

Indiana Voices: Herbert and Charlotte Read

Herbert and Charlotte Read

Trent Albert

Matt Williams

Porter County residents Charlotte and Herbert Read have spent their entire adult lives working to protect the Indiana Dunes and other aspects of the state's natural environment. Charlotte is a past executive director of the Save the Dunes Council and co-founder of the Hoosier Environmental Council and Herbert grew up in the Dunes—his parents' home is now on the National Register of Historic Places. Among the couple's many honors are the 2010 Indiana Conservation Hall of Fame Award as "preservers of Indiana's natural and cultural heritage" and the 2013 Izaak Walton League of America's Hall of Fame Award for their "commitment to conservation and ensuring outdoor America's future."

"We got married in 1952, the year Save the Dunes Council was established. In fact, our first check on our joint account went to the Save the Dunes Council.

"We lived across from the boundary of the Indiana Dunes State Park for a long time and our kids considered the state park a big front yard. We spent time there visiting the beach and had a favorite picnic spot in the woods.

"The geographical and geological nature of the Indiana Dunes is not duplicated anywhere else in this world. It ranks fourth in native plant diversity among the national parks. Per acre, it's No. 1. Schools bring children here and they find this great natural wonder, in some cases only 10 to 15 miles from their homes.

"Human beings cannot survive living only in overcrowded cities. Spiritually speaking, they have to have open space, whether it's farmland, forests, lakes or beaches. Open space is a resource we must preserve.

"Dunes are beautiful natural resources, but they're fragile, and too much incorrect use denigrates them. We want to see this globally significant area continue to be protected and preserved forever. There's a lot of work still to do to protect our resources. It never ends."

Calm waters are framed by a nearly cloudless sky at Indiana Dunes State Park near Chesterton. The southern shoreline of Lake Michigan includes both the State Park in Porter County and the Indiana Dunes National Lakeshore, which spans from Gary to Michigan City. Together, these two parks encompass more than 17,000 acres of beaches, dunes, wetlands, prairies and forests.

An otter greets a visitor to Muscatatuck National Wildlife Refuge in Jackson County.

An American lotus flower at Patoka River National Wildlife Refuge and Management Area in Gibson and Pike Counties

"What geography can give all Middle Westerners, along with the fresh water and topsoil, if they let it, is awe for an Edenic continent stretching forever in all directions.

"Makes you religious. Takes your breath away."

~ Kurt Vonnegut

Indiana Voices: Ned Cunningham

Ned Cunningham, Stinesville, is the head carver at Bybee Stone Co. in Ellettsville, which specializes in limestone fabrication and carving. The company provided the limestone to repair the Pentagon after the 9/11 attack. Cunningham has carved limestone for projects including the Palladium in Carmel, Chicago's Centennial Park, Duke University's Divinity School, the Seattle Art Museum and the Vintner's Guild in London.

Lisa Hendrickson

Ned Cunningham

"My father's father was a quarryman, and my dad became a limestone draftsman at a major mill here. I work with my dad, who is 85.

"I never dreamed I'd end up working in a limestone mill for 26 years. I was a figure model at Rhode Island School of Design and a professor said, 'You have a good sense of form, come take my stone class.' The first time I carved it was like, 'Oh, this is what love feels like.' I came back home and got a degree from IU in fine arts.

"It takes a terrific hand-eye coordination and mental focus to carve limestone—you have to be concentrating hard on what you're doing all the time, because you can't glue it back on. I taught myself how to work left-handed as well as right-handed. It's been a real boon to me.

"On a microscopic level, limestone is sort of like a porcelain sponge. It's full of pores, so in essence it breathes. It's the most easily worked stone because it's so homogenous. There's no grain to it; you can cut it in any direction; you can hand-sand it. It will take a lot of abuse during the fabrication process.

"This area used to be an inland sea, and we just happen to have a layer—the Salem Deposit— where some of the best limestone in the world is, that rises up near the surface in a 50-mile strip from Stinesville to Paoli.

"Limestone came back into vogue for building after the energy crisis of the 1970s when we realized that the heating and cooling advantages of a curtain wall of stone were huge. The energy input for fabrication is low, and it's fire retardant.

"People say, 'Isn't limestone carving a dying art?' And I say, 'No—walk around the IU campus.' But the fabrication process has changed a lot. Robots are here to stay, and we use digital scans, but there will always be a need for a human hand."

INFact

Indiana's State Stone

Most Hoosier courthouses and many university buildings are built of Indiana limestone. Other well-known buildings constructed of the official state stone:

- Biltmore Estate, Asheville, N.C.
- Empire State Building, New York City
- Lincoln Memorial, Washington, D.C.
- Metropolitan Museum of Art, New York City
- The Pentagon, Washington, D.C.
- Rockefeller Center, New York City
- United States Holocaust Memorial Museum, Washington, D.C.
- University of Chicago Neo-Gothic structures, Chicago
- National Cathedral, Washington, D.C.
- Yankee Stadium, New York City

Brian Wood

Sunset at Eagle Marsh in Fort Wayne

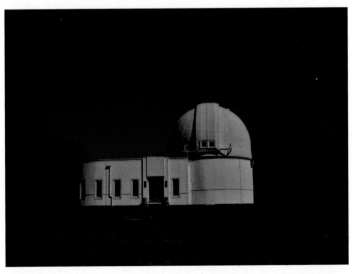

Shari Wagner

The Goethe Link Observatory in Morgan County was built in 1939 by the surgeon Dr. Goethe Link, an amateur astronomer. Now jointly owned by Indiana University and the Indiana Astronomical Society, it offers programs for stargazers.

Robert N. Anderson

Each fall, about 10,000 greater sandhill cranes stop at the marshes of Jasper-Pulaski Fish & Wildlife Area after feeding in nearby farmlands. It's the largest concentration of such sand-hills east of the Mississippi River.

A Good Place

Just before you get to the bridge,
where the river spills over the rocks
and begins to turn smooth again,
and the bank is lined with willows –

that would be a good place to stop,
and rein in the horse, and sit there
for a minute or two, listening
to the crickets and the bullfrogs.

You could look out at the fireflies
on the far shore, their movements
through the trees indistinguishable
from their reflections on the water.

With a nudge, the horse would start
onto the planks. As though your need
to cross had been acknowledged,
the old timbers would begin to sway.

Ahead, in the dark, there would be
birds fluttering among the rafters,
and all the night creatures calling,
and the river flowing beneath you.

~ Jared Carter

"A Good Place" originally appeared in the "Tipton Poetry Journal," published by Brick Street Poetry Inc. in Zionsville.

The Milky Way illuminates the night sky and Hoosier farmland.
David A. Plumier Jr.
Indiana State Department of Agriculture 2014 Photo Contest winner

By Philip Gulley

I was in the fourth grade, in Mrs. Betty Conley's class, when I first remember hearing the word *Hoosier*. I'm certain I heard it before then, but that was the first time the word stuck. We learned about the state bird—cardinal, the state tree—Liriodendron tulipifera, and the state stone—limestone. In the fifth grade, we moved on to U.S. history, but for one glorious year we dwelled on all things Indiana.

Mrs. Conley was an evangelist for the small town, believing its citizens possessed a degree of nobility lacking in city dwellers. When anything bad happened in our town, she blamed it on people from the city. So for the first 29 years of my life, I avoided Indianapolis like the plague, then was wooed there by its siren song. Unlike the Greek tragedies, my time there ended well. I only moved back to my hometown because I fell in love with a house that had a woodstove in the kitchen, which was, and remains, my idea of high living.

I've lived in Indiana for 55 of her 200 years, have traveled in every one of her 92 counties, speaking in libraries and churches, and can report, with a high degree of confidence, that there is no such thing as the Hoosier identity, if by identity we mean a common trait shared by all. Hoosiers are no more all the same than are Californians, Iowans or Texans. This isn't to say most of us don't aspire to a collective goal, in this case Hoosier hospitality. Just as a cowboy lurks in most Texans, so does the wish to be friendly dwell in most Hoosier hearts. In our 199th year, our Legislature voted in a law perceived to be unkind to gays and lesbians and such an outcry was raised by Hoosiers the politicians had to run for cover. We Hoosiers can be contrary, slow to change, and impossible to lead, but once we get it in our minds to welcome someone there's no stopping us.

continued

See page 248 for page 32 photo credits.

I've been fired twice in my life, once by a man from Oregon who tossed me overboard to the sharks, and the other time by a Quaker meeting in Indiana whose elders held my hand and wept as they eased me out the door. I returned the next month for a pitch-in dinner and they ushered me to the front of the line and slipped me an extra piece of pie. I'd like to think it was because they were Quakers, but now I believe it was the Indiana in them, that part of us that can't bear to be the cause of someone else's distress, however slim our fault. I once wrote a letter to a man newly arrived to our state, apologizing for its lack of an ocean.

In Indiana, guilt runs a close second to hospitality. We feel guilty about everything. I majored in theology at Marian University in Indianapolis, which was actually a four-year course of study in things I should feel bad about. William Henry Harrison, a governor of the Indiana territory-turned-president, died on his 32nd day in office, throwing the nation into a tizzy about presidential succession. Mrs. Conley told us his last words were, "I wish to apologize for causing you all this trouble." I think she made that up, because no one knows what he said, though it sounds like something a dying Hoosier would do, apologize for something he couldn't help.

Or maybe he could have helped it, had he not violated another maxim dear to Hoosiers—wash your hands. That's the third thing every Hoosier learns. First, be nice; second, be ready to apologize; third, always wash after shaking hands. But William Henry Harrison forgot, caught a cold, which led to pneumonia, which led to his death, which led to John Tyler being sworn in as president. That led to the annexation of Texas and its eventual inclusion as a state, for which we Hoosiers would like to apologize.

> "We Hoosiers can be contrary, slow to change, and impossible to lead, but once we get it in our minds to welcome someone there's no stopping us."

I'll be the first to admit that my love affair with Indiana has had its ups and downs. Whenever our Legislature meets, I think of leaving Indiana, but I stay put, mostly because of the woodstove in my kitchen and because my hero, Eugene Debs, was a Hoosier, born in Terre Haute on Nov. 5, 1855. It was Eugene Debs who said to the judge after being convicted of violating the Sedition Act in 1918, "I am opposing a social order in which it is possible for one man who does absolutely nothing that is useful to amass a fortune of hundreds of millions of dollars, while millions of men and women who work all the days of their lives secure barely enough for a wretched existence."

The judge was unimpressed and sentenced Debs to 10 years in prison, where he ran for president in 1920 and received nearly a million write-in votes. But, and here's the bright spot, Hoosiers had the good sense to elect Eugene Debs to the Indiana General Assembly in 1884. Any state that would elect Eugene Debs to public office has something noble, something virtuous, in its DNA. That nobility might well be a recessive gene, only popping up every now and then, but I intend to stick around to see if it emerges again.

When I was in the fourth grade, Mrs. Conley, that lover of all things Indiana, recited from memory Eugene Debs' 1918 speech before the federal court. Even now, I recall that wintry day, his glorious words warming our room and stirring our hearts, thinking that if Indiana never gave the world another gift, at least we had given it Eugene Debs.

Philip Gulley is a Quaker pastor and writer and speaker from Danville.

> "... And there's Gene Debs—a man 'at stands
> And jest holds out in his two hands
> As warm a heart as ever beat
> Betwixt here and the judgment seat!"
> ~ James Whitcomb Riley,
> "Regarding Terry Hut"

What's a "Hoosier"?

No one knows for sure where the term originated, but it was in use just a few decades after Indiana became a state. First spelled "Hoosher," it later transformed into "Hoosier." John Finley wrote a poem called "The Hoosher's Nest" in 1833. He later became mayor of Terre Haute.

Excerpts from "The Hoosher's Nest"

I'm told, in riding somewhere west,

A stranger found a *Hoosher's nest*,

In other words, a buckeye cabin,

Just big enough to hold Queen Mab in,

Its situation low, but airy,

Was on the borders of a prairie,

And fearing he might be benighted,

He hailed the house, and then alighted:

The Hoosher met him at the door,

Their salutations soon were o'er;

He took the stranger's horse aside,

And to a sturdy sapling tied;

Then having stripped the saddle off,

He fed him in a sugar-trough.

The stranger stooped to enter in,

The entrance closing with a pin,

And manifested strong desire,

To seat him by the log-heap fire,

Where half-a-dozen *Hoosheroons*,

With mush-and-milk, tin cups and spoons,

White heads, bare feet, and dirty faces,

Seemed much inclined to keep their places.

But madam, anxious to display

Her rough but undisputed sway,

Her offspring to the ladder led,

And cuffed the youngsters up to bed.

Invited shortly to partake

Of venison, milk, and Johnny-cake,

The stranger made a hearty meal,

And glances round the room would steal.

One side was lined with divers garments,

The other spread with skins of "varments,"

Dried pumpkins overhead were strung,

Where venison hams in plenty hung; ·

Two rifles placed above the door,

Three dogs lay stretched upon the floor;

In short, the domicil was rife

With specimens of *Hoosher* life.

~ *John Finley*

Roberts Settlement

Students stand before School House #5 in Roberts Settlement in Hamilton County in 1913. The settlement was founded in 1835 by free blacks of mixed racial heritage who migrated from the South to escape deteriorating racial conditions. Since 1924, a Roberts Settlement Homecoming has been held every Fourth of July weekend on the Roberts Settlement grounds. The community was one of many black farming settlements established in Indiana before the Civil War. The Greenville Settlement in Randolph County, founded in 1822, was the site of Union Literary Institute, one of the first racially integrated schools in the state.

La Porte County Historical Society

The La Porte County Fair is Indiana's oldest county fair, first sponsored by the La Porte County Agricultural Association in 1845. This photo, taken near the fair's "Wild West Show," is from 1903.

Kate Wehlann, The Salem Leader-Democrat

Members of the Society of the War of 1812 in the State of Indiana take part in a ceremony in Salem honoring the sacrifices of local soldiers who fought in the war.

Eddie Relick

Kids scramble for treats at the Bloomington Fourth of July parade.

Zhixiang Yang

Members of the Indianapolis Metropolitan Police Motorcycle Drill Team take part in the Indianapolis 500 Festival Parade each May. The team has performed at six U.S. presidential inaugural parades, as well as many festivals, schools, hospitals and nursing homes.

Picturesque fall foliage and covered bridges bring thousands of sightseers to Brown County every autumn.

Edward M. Wheeler

The popularity of craft beer draws Hoosiers to tasting rooms like this one at People's Brewing Co. in Lafayette.

Vincent Walter

The CISA Gallery in Hammond began sponsoring Arte Muerte, its annual Day of the Dead celebration, in 2005. Commonly observed in regions of southern Mexico, Day of the Dead pays tribute to deceased loved ones with art, music and food.

Thomas Semesky

Indiana Voices: Ginger Saccomando

Ginger Saccomando owns Wagner's Village Inn in Oldenburg, Franklin County.

"My family-owned business was established here in 1968. Through the last 47 years we have served many people from all over, but our most prized customers are locals. Over the years a lot of them have become like family, coming to share their special events like birthdays and anniversaries.

"We take pride in giving our hard-working and friendly Hoosier customers a place to sit and visit while our staff serves them our famous pan-fried chicken 'family style.'

"It means a lot for us to be able to provide a place for our locals to come and have fried chicken 'just like grandma made.'"

Hoosier Sugar Cream Pie

Sugar cream pie may trace its heritage in Indiana back to 1816, the year of Indiana statehood. Early Indiana pioneers and Amish bakers adopted it as an easy and delicious dessert, a tradition that Hoosiers still embrace today. This version is courtesy of Nick's Kitchen in Huntington.

Ingredients:

2 cups heavy cream

1/2 cup all-purpose flour

1/2 cup brown sugar

1/2 cup sugar

3 tablespoons sugar, for sprinkling

1/2 cup whole milk

1 teaspoon vanilla

1 (9-inch) pie crust

1 tablespoon unsalted butter

1 teaspoon ground cinnamon

Recipe Instructions:

1. Preheat oven to 350 degrees.
2. In a medium bowl, combine heavy cream, flour, brown sugar, 1/2 cup granulated sugar, milk, and vanilla.
3. Fit crust into a 9-inch pie pan and dot bottom with butter. Pour filling into crust. Combine cinnamon and remaining 3 tablespoons sugar and sprinkle on top. Bake pie until set and center is firm to touch, about 1 hour. Cool on a wire rack.

Perry Hammock, Indiana Bicentennial Commission

Nick's Kitchen in Huntington is said by many to be the birthplace of the breaded pork tenderloin, the unofficial sandwich of Indiana.

Elkhart County Convention and Visitors Bureau

A plethora of Hoosier pies

Bianca Lea

The taste of summer in Indiana

Daniel A. Baker

The Coney Island Wiener Stand in Fort Wayne, established in 1914, has been operated by descendants of the same Macedonian family since 1916. In 2014, it sponsored a coney-eating contest in celebration of its 100th anniversary.

Corn dogs are a favorite treat at the Indiana State Fair.

John Whalen

Indiana Voices: Cer Iang and Emily Sung

Indiana is home to more than 17,000 native Burmese, with Indianapolis having the largest population of recent Burmese immigrants of any city in the United States. Cer Iang, her daughter Emily Sung—a Lilly Endowment Scholar at Indiana University—and their family are members of the Chin tribe, one of more than 100 recognized Burmese ethnic groups.

"In 2009 our family fled Burma to escape the military dictatorship. We are Christian, and life was very difficult for us there. We did not have access to education and other opportunities.

"After living in Malaysia for two years, we came to the United States. We moved to Indianapolis, where we stayed at a relative's house for a few weeks. We met a lady who realized we didn't have anything. She made a telephone call, and the next day strangers came with a truck full of clothing, chairs and a TV. The next day they came back and brought us a lot of food. They were strangers, but they welcomed us with that level of care and love. We always pray for that family. May God bless them.

John Whalen

Cer Iang and Emily Sung

"The first thing we noticed when we came to Indianapolis is that the Chin community is bigger than any other city in the nation. That makes us feel at home. And despite the fact that we come from different backgrounds, people here are very understanding and welcome us. Our children are getting a very good education and there are so many resources, including the Burmese American Community Institute in Indianapolis, which offers volunteer and summer-research opportunities, homework assistance, leadership training and more. Indiana is a place that is helping us achieve our dreams."

Hong Yin

Chinese dragons march in the annual Indianapolis 500 Festival Parade.

▌NFact

Recent Immigrants

Immigrants obtaining residency status in Indiana in 2012 came from many countries. These are the top 10:

1. Burma
2. Mexico
3. India
4. China
5. Philippines
6. Nigeria
7. Thailand
8. United Kingdom
9. Vietnam
10. Canada

Source: U.S. Department of Homeland Security

A 100th birthday celebration in Greencastle. As of the publication of the 2010 U.S. Census, 1,083 centenarians lived in Indiana.
Marvetta Bee

Relay team members transfer the baton at the 2014 Indiana Special Olympics summer games.
Lesley Ackman

Grandfather and grandson share a milkshake at a Columbus restaurant.
Shannon Malanoski

Indiana Voices: Harriet Sweedler Miller

Harriet Sweedler Miller is a founding member of The Fort Wayne Women's Bureau, a nonprofit human services organization. Miller, who has three adult children and four grandchildren, has been in a committed relationship with Monica Wehrle for 38 years. They married in 2014.

Madeleine Ohrn

Harriet Sweedler Miller (left) and Monica Wehrle

"Over the past five decades, we have worked at the local and national level, creating agencies and events like the Fort Wayne Women's Bureau and the Run, Jane, Run: Women in Sports events. We provided consulting services to not-for-profit agencies through our company, Harmony Associates. We signed on as plaintiffs on the ACLU of Indiana same-sex marriage case. We stood up, spoke out, worked for social change.

"A few Fort Wayne women—suffragist and library founder Emerine Holman Hamilton, her granddaughter and pioneer in industrial diseases, Dr. Alice Hamilton, and civic leader Minnette Baum—were my heroes.

"These women represent the Hoosier values I hold most dear: finding and implementing solutions to problems that oppress powerless groups such as women, children, people of color, LBGT, single parents and the poor.

"Empowered by the example set by past generations of Hoosier women, we encourage our own families to continue the tradition of working for the common good. The next generation has accepted the challenge, each in their own way, focusing on their causes. I am both humbled and proud to be a part of the continuum of strong Hoosiers who have contributed their efforts to make Indiana an ideal place to foster equality, social justice and the love of family."

Indiana Humanities

A group of young girls draws their favorite Indiana meal at the Indiana Humanities Food for Thought exhibit during the Indiana Black Expo Summer Celebration. Indiana Black Expo, founded in 1970, sponsors both the Summer Celebration and the fall Circle City Classic in downtown Indianapolis.

The town of Friendship hosts the annual National Muzzle Loading Rifle Association and Old Mill Flea Market, highlighting the state's Early American culture with classes on traditional crafts, dulcimer music and instruction on shooting a muzzle-loading rifle.

Indiana Voices: Michael Pace

Michael Pace is a member of the Lenape tribe who educates Hoosiers about the contributions of his people to Indiana in the period when the state was being formed.

"Although the Lenape Tribe originally lived on the East Coast, southern New York, all of New Jersey and in eastern Pennsylvania, as the tribe was forced further west, we arrived in Indiana after 1795. My great-great-great-grandfather, Chief Anderson, whose Lenape name was 'Kithawenend,' founded the Madison County town that bears his name. The towns of Muncie and Strawtown were also founded by the Lenape.

"Since my retirement I have had the pleasure of working for Conner Prairie interactive historical park as an interpreter specialist to relate the story of the Lenape People in Indiana just before and after Indiana became a state in 1816. The Lenape, or Delaware, tribe was one of the many tribes to occupy this state.

"When the Lenape lived here, it was a low point for the tribe spiritually and it was a time of suffering, but from that point forward the Lenape have regained the legacy left to us by our forefathers.

"Today the Lenape Tribe is the 25th largest tribe in the United States. The spirit of the Lenape still dwells here today in Indiana and our contribution to statehood remains."

Michael Pace

Dianne Conrad Stoner Gustin

Firefighters in Peru salute those who have served their country.

Ken Kosky

The Valparaiso Popcorn Festival has been a late-summer draw for residents of northwest Indiana for almost 40 years.

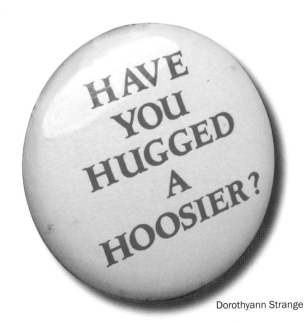

HAVE YOU HUGGED A HOOSIER?

Dorothyann Strange

James Whitcomb Riley and Theodore Roosevelt impersonators are in full costume at the annual Riley Festival in Greenfield. The October event celebrating the birthday of Riley, the "Hoosier poet," features a craft festival and the decades-old Parade of Flowers, in which elementary students march downtown to place bouquets of flowers around Riley's statue.

Sarah E. Kesterson

Fun on the Ferris wheel at the Dale Fall Festival in Spencer County.

Chris Ferguson

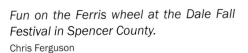

45

Indiana Voices: Greg Fehribach

Luke Woody

Greg Fehribach with his wife Mary Beth at their downtown Indianapolis home.

Greg Fehribach is an Indianapolis attorney and has served as an Americans with Disabilities Act consultant for a variety of high-profile projects, including the U.S. Capitol Visitors Center.

"Indiana has been home to my family for more than five generations. As a Hoosier with a physical disability, I have enjoyed educating others about how they can embrace their individualism while at the same time connecting equally with their neighbors. The removal of physical barriers from our iconic landmarks has been a catalyst for making those connections and overcoming the perceived obstacles that can come with a physical disability.

"Removing barriers makes Indiana a place that people with disabilities can truly call home. My home is a place where I can welcome friends new and old and foster a discussion about the importance of giving everyone a shot at independence. From Indiana's shining, accessible basketball arenas, to its inclusive, mowed football fields and its moonlit, barrier-free museums of history, I appreciate my accessible Hoosier home."

A Saturday night sing-along in Brown County

Dorothyann Strange

The holiday lights strung from the top of the Indiana Soldiers and Sailors Monument have delighted the multitudes who have attended the city's annual Circle of Lights festival since 1962. It's the largest man-made Christmas tree in the world, with nearly 5,000 lights strung by volunteer electrical workers.
Mary G. Feeney

Students take part in a day of service at Bethel College in Mishawaka.
Peter Ringenberg, Bethel College

Wedding celebration on a Brown County farm
Dorothyann Strange

Two friends at the Monroe County 4-H Fair

Lunchtime tamales at Mi Tierra Mexican restaurant in Roselawn, Newton County

The Athenaeum/Das Deutsche Haus in downtown Indianapolis was founded by German immigrants in the 1890s as a "house of culture" for mind and body. Listed on the National Register of Historic Places, it continues to be a community gathering spot today, including for its annual Oktoberfest celebration.

A Prost to Our Roots

When we came here, we were full of dreams and we did not let harsh reality kill them. We buried too soon too many of our young and elders but kept working, clearing, planting, praying in German. If our prayers were in German, our ambition was American: good land, a house we built with our hands of timber we cut down with an axe, crops in fields we cleared and plowed, cattle in barns. A church we built of Indiana sandstone pulled on sleds by oxen from a farm beside the Patoka River, near the bridge and the mill we took over built by Scots-Irish Presbyterian. Some of them moved on when we came in. The Croatian missionary Rev. Kundek, who spoke our native language, but not so well as us, sold us government land, looked after our needs, marched like a general at the head of our parades, built our court house, advised us how to vote and do business to stay together as a small German Catholic colony. The Benedictines from Einsiedeln, Switzerland took over for the Little General when he died. We built factories in which we made chairs, desks, fine cabinets, organs and pianos. The love of music has always been with us, even when shade from the forest still flooded in through our windows and open cabin doors.

Now we have brick houses, straight streets, vegetables growing in gardens, flowers blooming in beds surrounding our houses and in boxes hanging on the railings of the concrete bridge over the Patoka. Our Strassenfest celebrates our heritage in red, gold, and black and polkas in the summer. The church bells in our landmark Romanesque church with the Tower of London still peal and toll in the center of town. Basketball hoops hang from every garage. We keep our cemeteries well cut and trimmed and care for our ancestors' tombstones carved in German script with the names of the Bavarian and Baden towns they came from and wanted us to remember. We know where we came from but love it here where we stayed. Some of our young have learned how to speak the old tongue that was verboten during two world wars, and we have a sister city in southern Germany, a little town from which some of our ancestors came. We go there, they come here. Our taverns serve frosted schooners of beer that go down easy in the summer and we like our schnapps in the winter. A Prost to our roots all these years later!

~ Norbert Krapf
Indiana Poet Laureate 2008-2010

By Mauri Williamson

In order to properly define the Indiana farmer and his role in the history of our state, I must go back a few thousand years before the appearance of mankind. That spot on our earth called Indiana is located about 40 degrees north of the equator, ideal for farmers and their crops. We have days and nights, seasons, rains and droughts, all conducive to the growth of plants and animals. Add millennia to the recipe, along with rivers, lakes, forests and catastrophes, and throw in a few cold times, warm times and huge glaciers to clear off some boulders. Include some coal and minerals for good measure. And what do you have? "Indiana," a wonderful place to farm.

Add a native population who have lived here for several thousands of years and held things together, and you have a wonderful measure for success. Nature and time did the rest.

Humans of all kinds and abilities came upon the land to complete the formula. Restless explorers came to our shores and added much to the existing civilization. European societies brought farming techniques and the

continued

Autumn sunset on a Bartholomew County farm
Joanna M. Tucker

Indiana Voices: Larry Mitchell

Since 1976, the Indiana State Department of Agriculture has honored more than 5,000 Hoosier Homesteads—those farms that have remained in the same family for 100, 150 or 200 years—including the Muncie farm of sixth-generation farmers Larry and Vickie Mitchell.

"It is an honor to be the recipient of an inheritance passed down through the family. The house we live in, a New England saltbox, was built in 1860 and we are the sixth generation to live there. We have parcels dating back to 1839 and 1853. Our children are the seventh generation to live on the farm.

"I was bitten very early by the love of farming and animals. I have known since I was 6 years old that's what I wanted to do. In our family, we have always had off-farm jobs. My father was a county prosecutor. I taught fourth grade for 40 years. So it takes a family effort. When my parents were living, we had 275 acres with their land, and a cow and calf operation. It took the help of my parents, my wife and my children to make it successful, and it will take the work of my grandchildren, too, to make our farm successful in the future.

"People like to know how their food is raised. It's very important to have healthy animals. We raise beef cattle and have quite a menagerie of animals. People like to come by and observe farm life, and one of the things we've been able to do is bring children out to the farm. We hosted 52 class parties during my tenure as a teacher. My daughter teaches a special-needs class and we've been able to bring them out. That's the fun part: being ambassadors of agriculture.

"God isn't making any more land, so we have to be good stewards and make sure we pass it on to the next generation. We want to leave the land in better condition than we received it. It's been a blessing to have had it in our family."

Family members, from left, Luke Powers, 6, Larry Mitchell, Izabella Mitchell, 12, Vickie Mitchell, Isaac Mitchell, 5, Sarah Parker (holding baby Annabelle Parker) and Dustin Parker sit in front of the barn at the Mitchell Farms in Muncie. Mitchell Farms, which was established in 1839, is currently home to the sixth, seventh and eighth generation of family members.

More than 3,000 Indiana pork producers raise hogs, including this pair at Letsinger Farms in Tipton County. Pork production contributes more than $3 billion annually to the Indiana economy.

Grandpa and his pig

Old and new increasingly exist side-by-side on Indiana landscapes, like this traditional White County barn next to a modern-day wind farm.

Indiana farms, like Scott Farms in Carroll County, are family enterprises passed down through generations.

Indiana ranks fourth in the United States in soybean production, harvesting 223 million bushels on 5.15 million acres across the state, as on this Jay County farm.

White County squash

Marsha Williamson Mohr

Greta M. Scodro

Farmer's markets bring fresh produce to urban customers.

NFact

Indiana Popcorn Production

- 2nd largest popcorn producer in U.S.
- 91,000 acres of corn used to make popcorn

Source: National Agricultural Statistics Service

Indiana Humanities

$31.2 billion

Total direct value of sales for all Indiana agriculture-related industries in 2012. The economic ripple effects of these sales—which refer to supply chain purchases and the household spending of workers—generated another $12.9 billion in sales. Add these effects together, and agriculture's total impact on sales was an estimated $44.1 billion in 2012.

Source: Indiana Business Research Center

57

Indiana Voices: Neil Mylet

Neil Mylet is a farmer near Camden in Carroll County. The Purdue University graduate also holds five patents for technology products designed to help farmers work and learn.

"Each day while I'm working on the farm with my family I try to keep a camera within arm's length. I take photographs as a way to remind myself and others of how fortunate we are to live in such a wonderful state. The photographs that I capture are of simple things: sunrises, sunsets, tractors, fields, animals, streams, forests and the people that work in agriculture — the things that make Indiana special.

"For the last two centuries Indiana has been defined by hard-working people who are innovative and use their passion for agriculture to improve productivity. Technology has made a profound impact on the way farms operate in the 21st century. As I sit in the tractor, my source of inspiration comes from the same place generations before have garnered it: from a deep-rooted connection to the land and witnessing the breathtaking views of Indiana's scenic landscapes."

Thomas S. Campbell

Neil Mylet

Neil Mylet

Indiana ranks fifth in the nation for corn production. Livestock, poultry and dairy farmers are field corn's biggest corn customers, but corn is also used for ethanol production, manufactured goods, cornstarch, corn oil and corn syrup.

Tom Duffy Photography

The livestock auction at Dinky's Auction Center in Montgomery, population 343, is a weekly Daviess County event.

TRPhotography

Amish farmers have preserved a way of farming—and life—in Indiana.

Michael Nossett

Bridgeton Mill in Parke County is nearly 200 years old and still operating, attracting visitors and producing more than 20,000 lbs. of stone-ground products for sale.

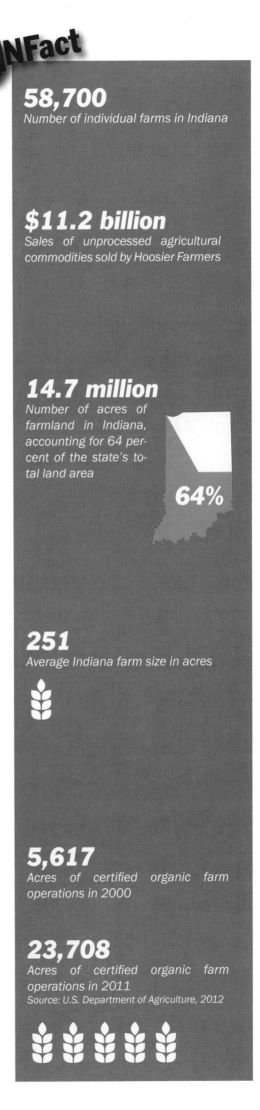

NFact

58,700
Number of individual farms in Indiana

$11.2 billion
Sales of unprocessed agricultural commodities sold by Hoosier Farmers

14.7 million
Number of acres of farmland in Indiana, accounting for 64 percent of the state's total land area

64%

251
Average Indiana farm size in acres

5,617
Acres of certified organic farm operations in 2000

23,708
Acres of certified organic farm operations in 2011
Source: U.S. Department of Agriculture, 2012

Indiana Voices: White Violet Center for Eco-Justice

Sister Ann Sullivan works at White Violet Center for Eco-Justice at Saint Mary-of-the-Woods, a ministry of the Sisters of Providence of Saint Mary-of-the-Woods.

"A commitment to the land has been a part of the history of the Sisters of Providence since the first six French Sisters of Providence, led by their foundress, Saint Mother Theodore Guerin, arrived in the Indiana woods in 1840. A sense of the land as 'home' and our responsibility to care for the land and its resources in sustainable ways have been a part of our history from the beginning.

"About 55 years ago our farm was a whole sustainable system. From grain for bread in our bakery to milk products from our dairy herd and chickens, this healthy system met the needs of our motherhouse community and honored the land in the process. This system changed as chemical agriculture became stronger after World War II. The farm became basically a grain farm, farmed with chemicals and large machinery. No livestock remained on our land.

"In 1993, the Sisters of Providence made the commitment to change that course of action by deciding that we would return our land to a sustainable organic state by certifying lands as organic, establishing gardens and orchards, and putting livestock back on our land to contribute to the system. Another component of the program is education for a just, sustainable future.

"Today, White Violet Center for Eco-Justice, a ministry of the Sisters of Providence, provides an avenue for people of all ages to delve into ecological justice through our vegetable share program, alpaca herd and fiber program, chickens, beehives, organic gardens and orchard. Thousands of people visit every year to tour and participate in regular educational workshops, eco-spirituality offerings, internships, sabbaticals and other special events."

Cheryl Casselman

Fiber workshops at White Violet Center for Eco-Justice help participants learn to use alpaca wool. The alpaca herd and fiber program, vegetable share program, beehives and orchard are a ministry of the Sisters of Providence of St. Mary-of-the-Woods.

Alpacas at the White Violet Center for Eco-Justice.
Cheryl Casselman

Kristie Spear, 2013 Indiana State
Department of Agriculture Photo Contest winner

Roadside stands are a frequent sight on Indiana back roads in the summer.

Tara R. Henry

George Henry and his daughter, Rachel Pfeiffer, next to their John Deere 4840 on the family farm in Waterloo Township, Fayette County. The farm has been in the family 100 years, growing corn, soybeans and raising nearly 100 head of cattle.

Holtkamp Winery

Holtkamp Winery is one of nearly 100 Indiana wineries, a growing industry for the state. Indiana also was home to the first successful commercial vineyard in the country in the late 1700s in Vevay.

Susie Richter, La Porte County Historical Society

The Door Prairie Barn just south of La Porte on Highway 35, built in 1882. Along with octagonal barns like this one, more than 200 multi-purpose round barns were built in Indiana from 1874 to 1936, with more than 100 still standing today.

Tom Duffy Photography

Boiling the maple sap at Maple Valley Farm in Ellettsville

American persimmon (Diospyros virginiana) is native to Indiana, traditionally foraged—never picked from its tree—and eaten in persimmon pudding, a Hoosier specialty.

Indiana has more than 600 acres of highbrush blueberries, ranking it 12th in the United States.

Hardworking 4-H youth display projects at the Elkhart County 4-H fair, one of the largest 4-H Fairs in the nation.

"Take Down," a 2014 Indiana State Department of Agriculture photo contest winner.

Technology is everywhere—including the farm.

David A Pluimer Jr.

A familiar face in Indiana   Steve Glaser

Vincent Walter

Originally established in 1949 as the Agronomy Farm, the Purdue Agronomy Center for Research and Education is located on 1,134 acres northwest of Purdue University.

Joni Montgomery

Nationally, Indiana ranks first in duck production, third in egg production and third in turkey production.

Somewhere Inside Me a Gray Barn Is Rising

I remember Indiana and riding with my grandmother
in her '57 Ford on the road to Lowell,
asking why the barns had names on them,
those sturdy gray bodies
rising through golden looms
of corn, the slow shuttle
of cattle lowing outside the open doors.

And that barn across the field
from the grammar school where we played
ball at recess, how sometimes
I'd go off alone, lean on the fence
and stare, Arthur's Knights and Vikings of the north
fighting it out in castles of hay.

That rule the teachers had
about never crossing the fence, the barn
always there, always outside
my reach.

It builds itself
now, as it has before,
in the shadows between things,

like the night in the cabin
in northern Colorado, rising there
in the scent of wet pine, the wooden silence
of water under the bridge building
on the flat of a stone that split the river
as it crossed into two paths,

like so many graveyard shifts
at the brickyard in East Chicago,
calloused hands of press operators, sweat
seeping through blue work-shirts
into the three a.m. lunchroom, their tired smiles
over coffee in the silence that hummed
inside steam drifting like small fragments
of some larger breath we all shared,

like that afternoon last fall, the tall
African student in that bulky fur coat
and white stocking cap, frightened
in the shuffle between classes,
how I wanted to reach out,
hold him, how I even dreamed about him,
and when I turned the next day
in the lunch line to tell Jim, he was there
again, behind him, holding a bowl of lettuce
and a soup spoon,
same coat and hat . . .

Out of the tall grass
the barn rises, rises beneath the maples,
within the solitude of shade, between
each worm-chewed leaf.

But the barn rises and falls
as we move.

Because we rarely know
the right words, because touching
only brings us just outside
our reach, because
we are only shadows drifting
beneath broad maple leaves
when the butterfly begins to sing us
in its sleep,

the barn shifts its tired feet
and sinks slowly
into layers
of phlox and maple.

~ George Kalamaras, Indiana Poet Laureate

Durnal Family Barn in Brown County
Dianna Wilson Photography

By Pete Buttigieg

The Hoosier state is full of open and pastoral landscapes, from the Indiana Dunes National Lakeshore to the banks of the Ohio River. One of the most iconic images of our state is one of a rusted basketball hoop on a family farm. While our agricultural heritage and development is widely known, the cities and towns of Indiana have long been their own marketplaces for economic and cultural exchange.

Indiana is a state that embraces its history, and our towns have always served as theaters to the past. When Indiana was a nascent territory, our first capital was Vincennes, along the border with Illinois. In 1813, the capital was relocated to Corydon, where it remained through statehood until being permanently moved to Indianapolis in 1825. More than 190 years later, our capital city is well established and growing. But those early relocations reinforce a feeling that Indiana's cities and towns have always been on the move.

With more industrialization and the mass commercialization of goods in the late 19th century and early 20th century, Indiana cities took a leading role in the American economy. Here in northern Indiana, Oliver Chilled Plow Works and the Studebaker Brothers Manufacturing Company became giants of enterprise by combining sound technical models with Indiana hard work. A couple of generations later, medical device companies around Warsaw and recreational vehicle builders throughout Elkhart County combined similar skills to become global leaders of design and production.

continued

The Robert N. Stewart Bridge frames the Bartholomew County Courthouse in downtown Columbus.
Mike Briner

Our growing small towns even became the proving grounds for social scientists studying the growing sense of Americana sweeping the country. Husband-and-wife sociologists Robert Staughton Lynd and Helen Merrell Lynd settled in Muncie to conduct experiments on community norms. They re-named the city in their work "Middletown," where they studied family, work, leisure, religion and local government in the years leading up to World War II.

The post-World War II decades brought major shifts to the Hoosier consciousness. Interstate highways were constructed in the 1950s and truly made our state the "Crossroads of America," linking the Midwest to the East, South and growing West. At the same time, our cities and towns were being transformed by these new roads and by physical expansion, demographic shifts, growth of the middle class and suburbanization.

In my hometown of South Bend, we have re-lived these transformations in thinking about civic service and governance. In 1963, a little less than 20 years before I was born, Studebaker closed, putting thousands out of work and leaving behind dozens of unused factory buildings. Over the last 50 years, South Bend has tried to rebuild and

> *"Through our people and good governance, we can create diverse communities of trust and healthy environments for job creation where people want to live, work and play."*

reimagine our sense of what it means to be a city in the aftermath of subtraction. Like countless other Hoosier communities facing hardships or recessions, we matched our strong values and hopes with dogged perseverance. A spring of renewal and recovery is flowing again in South Bend and other cities and towns across Indiana.

I believe our cities and towns can serve their residents, businesses and students well by focusing first on one major tenet: making sure that the basics are easy. Finding a job, raising a family, paying for college and starting a business are challenging enough without having to worry about safe drinking water, infrastructure improvements and safe neighborhoods. Through our people and good governance, we can create diverse communities of trust and healthy environments for job creation where people want to live, work and play.

On a broader level, the popularity of cities is on an upward trajectory. More Americans now live in cities than in rural environments. More young people and families are seeking communities where they can walk, bike, congregate, raise a family and retire. Farmer's markets are bustling and people are eating more local foods from our farms and drinking craft beverages from local shops. In an increasingly connected world, people are drawn more than ever to the interactions and social exchanges that can occur in a city. It is up to all of us to ensure that these places remain safe, unique, authentic and diverse.

Investments in people and places help all Hoosiers as we witness our changing urban landscapes, work together regionally, strive for bipartisanship and make disciplined fiscal decisions for the next generation. A prime example of this stewardship is Indiana Downtown, a program of the Indiana Association of Cities and Towns, which offers technical assistance for the revival of downtowns and town squares.

Angela Jones

The West Baden Springs Hotel, opened in 1902, sat empty for decades until it reopened in 2007 after a multi-million-dollar renovation made possible by Hoosier philanthropists Bill and Gayle Cook.

Re-appreciating and reusing old buildings and historical sites has become a movement across Indiana as we find timeless value in our architecture and identify new purposes for spaces. Madison's downtown is the largest contiguous National Historic Landmark in the United States, with 133 blocks of the downtown district preserved. Madison had the architect Frances Costigan, and Columbus became famous for its architecture thanks to industrialist J. Irwin Miller, who paid for distinguished architects to design buildings in his Bartholomew County city.

West Baden's famous West Baden Springs resort was once known as the "Eighth Wonder of the World" because the resort featured the largest unsupported dome in North America at the time. Here in South Bend, buildings and land that once held Studebaker factories now offer new wonders in the form of data centers and the new Notre Dame Turbomachinery Laboratory.

Matt Cashore

South Bend Mayor Pete Buttigieg offers a toast to the city of South Bend's 150th birthday at the Century Center on May 22, 2015.

Our state's bicentennial celebration comes in an age when cities and towns are on the move. While the Lynds' Middletown was a pseudonym and the fictitious Pawnee can only be seen on NBC's "Parks and Recreation," our real hometowns are crossroads of innovative industry, academia and student life, state-of-the-art medical care, and places of worship and distinct character.

As we reflect on the last 200 years of Indiana history, let us also think about the generations who will follow us. The poet Langston Hughes wrote that "We build our temples for tomorrow, strong as we know how." So it is with our cities and towns, as we shape them for the decades to come. Like people, cities and towns have personalities and character, and it is up to us to ensure that across Indiana, the character of our communities will continue to make us proud.

Pete Buttigieg is the mayor of South Bend.

The atrium of the West Baden Springs Hotel was once the largest unsupported dome in the world.

Rona Schwarz

Small towns such as Attica in Fountain County are trying to preserve their downtown business districts.

The Indiana Central Canal was envisioned as a way to connect the Wabash and Erie Canal to the Ohio River, but the canal project went broke and was stopped in 1839. This rebuilt section in downtown Indianapolis remains, and is an oasis in the heart of the city.

Mark Curry

An August moon shines on Henry Moore's "Large Arch" and the bell tower of Eliel Saarinen's First Christian Church in Columbus.

Indianapolis Museum of Art

The Columbus home of J. Irwin and Xenia Simons Miller, now known as Miller House and Garden, is one of the world's premiere showcases of Modernist architectural, landscape and interior design. Eero Saarinen, Alexander Girard and Dan Kiley collaborated with the Millers in the 1950s to create this home, now a National Historic Landmark owned by the Indianapolis Museum of Art.

J. Irwin Miller, the long-time chairman of Cummins Engine Co., subsidized the use of world-class architects in Columbus, turning the city into a widely recognized showcase of modern architecture.

The Indianapolis Star

Indiana Voices: Laura Yates

Laura Yates in front of Little Leaf

Hailey Preston

Hoosier housing styles have evolved for 200 years. Tiny, portable houses are relatively new and appeal to Laura Yates, a graduate student at Indiana University, Bloomington.

"I've always been inspired by those who build their lives around their values. A few years ago, I started the process of designing and building my tiny home, Little Leaf, around my values of financial and environmental health. I live full-time in my home in Greene County while pursuing a graduate education at Indiana University's School of Public and Environmental Affairs.

"Numerous people around the country, and in recent years, a growing number of Hoosiers, have chosen to live their values by building, designing and living in tiny homes. Historically, small homes and cabins have been the central hub of so many Hoosier families. Over the past century, the average family size has stayed roughly the same but the average house size has steadily increased. For a number of reasons—financial, family, environmental—many Hoosiers are passing on the opportunity to live in a large home, and are instead choosing to honor their roots and traditions by living in a smaller—or even a 'tiny'—home."

The Century of Progress District in Beverly Shores includes five houses barged across Lake Michigan to Indiana after the 1933 World's Fair in Chicago. This Florida Tropical House and the others are being restored by an innovative leasing partnership between Indiana Landmarks, the Indiana Dunes National Lakeshore and private individuals.

Todd Zeiger, Indiana Landmarks

Michael Gasper

The centerpiece of Indianapolis is the neoclassical Indiana Soldiers and Sailors Monument.

INFact

Smallest Indiana Towns

- *River Forest (Madison Co.), 22*
- *New Amsterdam (Harrison Co.), 27*
- *North Crow's Nest (Marion Co.), 46*
- *Laconia (Harrison Co.), 49*
- *Alton (Crawford Co.), 55*

Source: 2014 U.S. Census estimates

Largest Indiana Cities

- *Indianapolis (Marion Co.), 848,788*
- *Fort Wayne (Allen Co.), 258,522*
- *Evansville (Vanderburgh Co.), 120,346*
- *South Bend (St. Joseph Co.), 101,190*
- *Carmel (Hamilton Co.), 86,682*

Indiana Voices: Brittany Faith Young

Brittany Faith Young, 19, is the 2014-2015 Indiana FFA state president and a native of Hope.

"I love small towns. This year while traveling the state, I have driven through my share of them, but to me nothing can compare to my small hometown of Hope.

"In Hope, if you have a flat tire, it's more than likely someone will pull over to help you. If it's senior night for the basketball team, cheerleading squad and band, at least half of the town will show up to show its support. If a piece of farm equipment breaks down at 8:00 p.m. and there's still at least two hours of work required to finish up, all it takes is a quick call to your neighbor. Before you know it—with an extra pair of hands, some tools and a few prayers—you are back in the tractor finishing up that last field for the evening.

"Things like this happen in Hope, where the people have a heart the size of Texas. I honestly could not imagine *not* calling this small pinpoint of a town my hometown."

Terri Young

Brittany Faith Young welcomes visitors to Hope.

Lesley Ackman

The entire town of Story, which never recovered from the Great Depression, is now a country inn and bed and breakfast.

The Fowler Theatre opened in 1940 and was restored to its former neon, chrome and porcelain glory more than 60 years later by the Prairie Preservation Guild, which was created with help from Indiana Landmarks, a group dedicated to saving important Indiana places. The guild was founded expressly to save the structure and keep movies showing in the Benton County town. The theater remains open and is staffed by volunteers.

Nappanee, which straddles Elkhart and Kosciusko counties, celebrates its small-town vibe.

Indiana Voices: Judy O'Bannon

Judy O'Bannon served as Indiana's first lady from 1997 to 2003 and as chairwoman of Indiana's Main Street program for 10 years. She is host of the WFYI-TV program "Communities Building Community" and writes a biweekly column for The Corydon Democrat.

The Corydon Democrat

"Our communities are really a little like an old rag rug that we in Indiana are used to associating with everyday use. The rug is made up of the fabric of people's experiences—an old housedress, a favorite school skirt, a man's shirt—and you weave them together in a new way. They become a rug—something sturdy you can stand on, a foundation. I think that's a metaphor for the rich texture of life that comes from people doing things together, becoming intertwined with someone else in an experience in a community. All of the threads are important, but they're all different. Whether it's picking up trash along the road, bailing somebody out after a fire or going together and raising money to build a hospital, you have an emotional, an intellectual and a real physical connection.

"I've traveled to little towns all over the state. When folks do something in their hometown they are so energized. People would tell me, 'We cleaned up that lot and put a bench there.' Well, it's not earth-shattering, but in a way it is: that little park that they cleaned up—it changed them. It changed them inside and what they think about themselves, it changed how they relate to other people in the community—especially the ones who worked with them or those who opposed them—and it changed that community forever."

Interchanges like this one on Interstate 69 drew commerce and people away from small-town business districts.

Indiana Department of Transportation

René Stanley, Indiana Bicentennial Commission

Santa Claus, in Spencer County, celebrates its namesake 365 days a year and is home to the Holiday World amusement park, which claims the world's longest water coaster.

Irvington Historical Society

The Second Empire-style Benton House, built in 1873, is a symbol of Irvington, which was founded a few years earlier as a suburban enclave east of Indianapolis for artists, writers and other professionals. It was annexed by Indianapolis in 1901.

Flag-waving starts at a young age in Delphi in Carroll County.

Gail Baker Seest

Indiana Voices: Robert Vanlandingham

Small towns across America have been struggling for decades, their downtowns decimated by the changing shopping habits of consumers and an exodus of jobs and people. Hoosier small towns are no different, but some are reinventing themselves. Wabash, population 10,500, is a Hoosier success story, with a restored downtown and a civic spirit that Mayor Robert Vanlandingham says can be duplicated wherever neighbors are willing to work together. Now, tourists come to see live shows at The Honeywell Center (named for the company that has its roots in Wabash), they stay at the Charley Creek Inn, and they take in a movie at the renovated Eagles Theater. Tourism, which barely existed in Wabash before the recession, was a $42 million industry in 2013.

"I was an elementary school teacher and principal for 31 years. In that job I learned how to work with staff, students, their parents and a budget. Working in that position helped me acquire people skills. Those were skills that I needed in order to get our community to work together to create a vision.

"Working together has blossomed into something big. You can't do it by yourself...it takes the whole community. We work closely with our neighboring towns, talking frequently. You don't always get exactly what you want, but you work it out through compromise and cooperation.

"It takes a tremendous amount of energy to achieve your vision. I'm 76 and have developed strong friendships and professional relationships through the years, but when I want to get things accomplished, I get the younger professionals involved. They have the energy to carry the vision through."

Wabash Mayor Robert Vanlandingham in front of Marelli's Bloom Boutique, one of many small retailers that enliven the town center.

After years of disinvestment following World War II, downtown Indianapolis was transformed into a major destination for conventions and special events in the last decades of the 20th century.

Evansville's Four Freedoms Monument, opened in 1976, was built with four columns salvaged from an Evansville railroad depot that was built in 1882 and razed in 1961.

Indiana Voices: Karen Freeman-Wilson

Karen Freeman-Wilson is the former Indiana attorney general and is the mayor of Gary.

"Nestled on the shores of Lake Michigan, with beaches and dunes that rival some vacation destinations, Northwest Indiana has a rich and intriguing history. Of course, my first love is my hometown, Gary. Senior residents often share memories of Gary in its heyday complete with a bustling downtown area, a flourishing steel industry and an educational system that was the model for other districts around the country to follow.

"Gary will forever be in the history books for being home to Michael Jackson and the Jackson 5, electing the first black mayor of a midsized American city and more recently, electing me as its first female mayor.

"I say without hesitation that the best thing about Gary is its people. They're talented, passionate and, most of all, resilient. Gary also has a very strong faith community that continues to play a vital role in the city's revival. Many of the creative initiatives being implemented, such as urban gardens, park and vacant lot adoptions, and community cleanups are being spearheaded by churches.

"As one of the larger cities in Northwest Indiana, we are proud to represent the region as a diverse community that is committed to a better quality of life for all."

Geoffrey Black

John Whalen

Stewart House Urban Farm and Gardens, Gary, on the site of the former Stewart Settlement House, organized during the Depression to provide social services for Gary's black community.

Presidential candidate Sen. Robert F. Kennedy informs Indianapolis supporters of the assassination of the Rev. Martin Luther King Jr. on April 4, 1968. Upon learning of King's death, Kennedy dispensed with his prepared remarks and spoke off the cuff. His message of peace is thought to have played a role in Indianapolis being one of the few American cities that didn't explode in violence in the aftermath of King's assassination. The words below, taken from Sen. Kennedy's speech, are engraved on his memorial at Arlington National Cemetery.

Charles A. Berry, The Indianapolis Star

"Aeschylus ... wrote, 'Even in our sleep, pain which cannot forget falls drop by drop upon the heart, until, in our own despair, against our will, comes wisdom through the awful grace of God.'

"What we need in the United States is not division; what we need in the United States is not hatred; what we need in the United States is not violence and lawlessness; but is love and wisdom, and compassion toward one another, and a feeling of justice toward those who still suffer within our country, whether they be white or whether they be black."

~ Sen. Robert Kennedy, speaking in Indianapolis on April 4, 1968

Eric Schoch

The hands of Martin Luther King Jr. and Bobby Kennedy reach out from the Peace Memorial in King Park in Indianapolis.

Indiana Voices: Bill Taft

Bill Taft is executive director of the Indianapolis office of Local Initiatives Support Corp., a national organization working to renew communities across the country.

John Whalen

Bill Taft in Fountain Square, one of the neighborhoods his organization has helped get back on its feet.

"The old neighborhoods of Indianapolis are both a tremendous asset and daunting challenge for our community. These are the places that contain the most potential for urban growth and the greatest concentration of human misery in our city, and it is up to us to determine which truth will dominate their future. These neighborhoods are the community that I love, and I believe that it is my life labor, calling and pleasure to help these neighborhoods become truly vibrant and their residents participate fully in the economic, spiritual and social wealth of central Indiana.

"Since I was a child I have loved old places that wear their history on their sleeve. I believe old neighborhoods can build on the physical and cultural remnants of their past to become vibrant neighborhoods where people enjoy the best of true urban living. Residents should be able to walk and bike safely to many of their daily places while enjoying the benefits of knowing their neighbors and working to provide a good life for both their families and the larger community. In my 24 years of working in places like Fountain Square, Herron-Morton and the near east side, I have seen tangible elements of this vision achieved. I hope to spend the rest of my career helping more neighborhoods achieve their own version of this good life."

Rona Schwarz

Completed in 1929 at a cost of $2.5 million, the Scottish Rite Cathedral in downtown Indianapolis is one of the largest Masonic buildings in the world and is known for its intricate detail inside and out.

William J. Lackner

The Lanier Mansion, completed in 1844, is an anchor of the 130-block Madison Historic District, one of the largest such districts in the country.

Lockerbie Square, where many immigrants built their homes, is the oldest intact neighborhood in Indianapolis. The houses of Lockerbie were built in the mid- to late 19th century and range from vernacular cottages to high-style brick homes.

Michael Gasper

INFact

What's in a Name?

In Indiana...

- There are 5 Mt. Pleasants—in Cass, Delaware, Johnson, Martin and Perry counties.
- There are 4 Buena Vistas—in Franklin, Gibson, Harrison and Randolph counties.
- There are 4 Millersburgs—in Elkhart, Hamilton, Orange and Warrick counties.
- There are 4 Salems—county seat of Washington County, others in Adams, Jay and Union counties.
- There are 62 cities and towns that are NEW Something.
- There are 26 cities and towns that are MOUNT Something.
- There are 23 cities and towns that are SAINT Someone.
- There are 13 cities and towns that have GREEN, GREENE, or GREENS as first name or first syllable.
- There are 12 cities and towns that have LAKE as first name or syllable (two are in Lake County).

Source: Index of Cities and Towns, Indiana Transportation Map 2005

Molly Faber

Buckner Park has served the city of Fort Wayne in a variety of capacities, from public farmland to military training ground, since it was purchased by the city in 1969. Today, its spray pool offers relief on a hot summer day.

Bull's-Eye 20 Questions (Hoosier Edition)

By Will Shortz

Here's a test of your word "marksmanship." The answer to each of the 20 questions below is the name of one of the 21 Indiana cities and towns in the bull's-eye target. Each answer scores a "hit," which you may cross off in the target, since no name has been used more than once. When all the questions have been answered, the one name that remains will identify the Indiana city where I was born (8/26/1952).

Will Shortz

Donald Christensen

Will Shortz was born and raised on an Arabian horse farm in [answer to puzzle on this page]. He graduated from Indiana University in 1974 with the world's only college degree in enigmatology, the study of puzzles, which he designed himself through IU's individualized major program. Shortz is the crossword editor of The New York Times (since 1993), puzzlemaster for National Public Radio, founder/director of the American Crossword Puzzle Tournament and the author or editor of more than 500 books of puzzles.

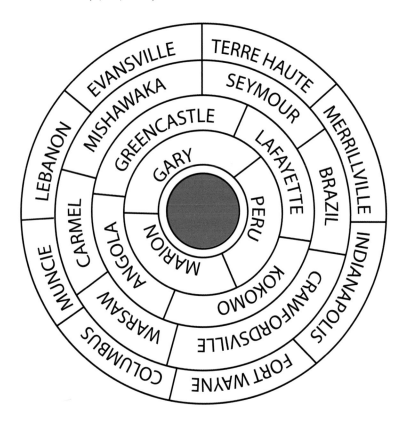

Which name...

1. is an anagram of VALVE LINES?

2. would name something sweet if you inserted an A in the middle?

3. sounds like what glasses help you do?

4. when read backward, spells a two-word phrase meaning "had not been cooked"?

5. uses only the 11th, 13th and 15th letters of the alphabet?

6. would name a color if you switched its middle two letters?

7. would name things seen in front of the Indianapolis Library if you changed two consecutive letters to a single N?

8. sounds like the words on a gift tag to the author of "Tom Sawyer"?

9. spells, when you read the letters in the odd positions in order from left to right, a word meaning "something very tasty"?

10. sounds roughly like a five-word sentence describing a large fourth letter of the alphabet surrounding a Macintosh computer?

11. contains a word meaning "sick" twice?

12, 13, 14 & 15. is the name of a country? [four answers]

16. when you put the second syllable first and pronounce the result, sounds like a synonym for "sailor"?

17. consists of the first two or three letters of four state names in order?

18. consists of a musical note inside a gift at a baby shower?

19. completes this punny sentence: Jethro and Sue Ann are _____ at church this weekend.

20. is an anagram of a word meaning "four-sided figures with parallel sides" + E?

Answers: 1. *Evansville* 2. *Carmel* (caramel) 3. *Seymour* (see more) 4. *Warsaw* (was raw) 5. *Kokomo* 6. *Gary* (gray) 7. *Columbus* (columns) 8. *Fort Wayne* (for Twain) 9. *Terre Haute* (treat) 10. *Indianapolis* (in D an Apple is) 11. *Merrillville* 12-15. (in any order) *Angola, Brazil, Lebanon, Peru* 16. *Muncie* (seaman) 17. *Mishawaka* (Missouri, Mississippi, Hawaii, Washington, Kansas) 18. *Lafayette* (la'FA yette) 19. *Marion* (marryin') 20. *Greencastle* (rectangles + E). I was born and raised in *Crawfordsville*.

Chicago looms in the background as the sun sets on the Michigan City Lighthouse in La Porte County.

New Harmony, in Posey County, was settled in the 19th century as a Utopian society. Its historic buildings and visitors' center, which opened in 1979, are a draw for tourists.

"The real game-changer will probably turn out to have been near-perfect Parkview Field and the phenomenal first year of the Fort Wayne TinCaps baseball team. That project started bringing more people downtown."

~ Fort Wayne News–Sentinel

Parkview Field, home of the Fort Wayne TinCaps baseball team, brought new life to downtown Fort Wayne after it opened in 2009.

Carmel, one of the most prosperous cities in the United States, has remade its downtown into the Carmel Arts & Design District.

"My No. 1 priority when I was mayor of Indianapolis, from 1975 to 1991, was to use government policy to attract people downtown. After all, you can't be a suburb of nothing. You don't want a city to be a donut with nothing in the center."

–William H. Hudnut III as quoted in the Chicago Tribune, Nov. 1, 1998

Indianapolis honored its longtime mayor in 2015 with the dedication of Hudnut Commons and the unveiling of a life-size statue.

Natalie Stubblefield

St. Joseph River

Compared to the Amazon, an overgrown brook,
Servile to industry, timid flooder, flows that skein
In shimmers, river that zigzags the shale plain
Like my late aunt's blind stitching when she took
Cognac for cramps. Downtown, a sharp crook
North toward the lake, weathered docks, the bane
Of gutted factories, boarded storefront, that eyestrain
I get driving on rust-belt roads that overlook
The coal-gray drifts, an occasional floater gored
By willow tusks, the last oak leaves taking flight, spun
In gusts, their tumultuous glide on lathing eddies,
Sawtooth ripples that portend more snow, the sword
Of ice rusting out iron piles, bridge where Adrian,
My son, fed the geese, then one day slid as if on skis,
                              Spring's blustery sprees,
Yet I quick enough, Thank God, to catch him before
The plank's edge. Late by one second, would tragedy's door
                              Have burst open, the floor
Of normalcy caving? Job would laugh at such a thing,
Like moths we hover over chaos, our lifeline a silk string.

~ Orlando Ricardo Menes

Originally published in "Fetish," the University of Nebraska Press, 2013.

By Barbara Olenyik Morrow

In the autumn of 1979 I left my home and a job in Louisville, Kentucky, steered my Ford Maverick across the Kennedy Bridge over the Ohio River, and headed up Interstate 65. In Indianapolis, I followed the I-465 beltway partway round the city, veered onto Interstate 69 and cruised northeast, past billboards and road signs and exit ramps, past unseen towns and acres of farmland. Thirty miles from the Michigan line, I pulled off the highway and drove to nearby Auburn. My new Indiana home—I had arrived at last.

At the time, I gave no thought to how earlier generations arrived in the Hoosier state. Turn the key in the ignition, press the pedal and go—such was my frame of reference on the subject of transportation. But the intervening years have given me opportunities to explore my adopted state. And with travel, I've come to appreciate the comings and goings of early inhabitants and the means by which they moved. Today, as I drive alongside the Wabash River southwest of Fort Wayne, I picture Native Americans in that liquid highway, paddling canoes to downstream villages or preparing to portage to the St. Mary's River. Elsewhere, on rivers such as the Kankakee or St. Joseph (South Bend), I imagine fur traders and missionaries and a French explorer or two. Early transportation in Indiana? I get it. Rivers ruled.

The Ohio River, of course, reigned as a vital highway. Pioneering families, having crossed the Alleghenies, waited out the winter in places such as Pittsburgh and then, when the river's ice washed away, they launched their flatboats—the decks filled with mules and cows and boisterous children. Did the youngsters ever holler "Are we there yet? Is that shore yonder Indiana?" Children being children, I suppose they did. And Lawrenceburg and Madison and Jeffersonville . . . well, that's how those Hoosier settlements, in part, came to be.

On the road to the future
Chris Ferguson

continued

The newcomers didn't always stay put. Through thick forests, across soggy wilderness, they sensed there was something they needed to see. And fertile land they needed to homestead. So they followed trails stamped out by migrating animals, most notably the Buffalo Trace from New Albany to Vincennes, and inched their way upward and westward through the state. So, too, did new arrivals inch their way across Indiana's midsection. By the 1830s, a steady parade of them—in oxcarts and Conestoga wagons, on horseback and on foot—made their way from Richmond to Indianapolis to Terre Haute along the nation's first federally funded highway, the National Road. Made of crushed stones and, in places, wood planks, the road was better than a bison path, but not always much better. Not with tree stumps protruding here and there and rainy seasons creating a muddy byway.

And if roads were impassable? I page through the writings of Mother Theodore Guerin and wince at descriptions of her head-bumping stagecoach journey north from Evansville in 1840: "We were again in the forest, and the ground was so covered with water that it was like a vast pond . . . Once the carriage struck a stumbling horse, and a wheel went over the trunk of a tree, and lo! the carriage was again thrown on its side . . . The water poured in on us. We thought we were surely gone."

Happily, Mother Theodore—who the Roman Catholic Church made a saint in 2006—and her companions survived, long enough to establish schools in Indiana, open two orphanages in Vincennes, care for countless sick, and found an academy today known as Saint Mary-of-the-Woods College. Happily, too, Hoosiers set about making primitive roads less primitive.

Even so, water transportation remained important, which explains why Hoosiers, in the early 1830s, went on a canal-building binge. With picks and shovels, hundreds of laborers, many of them Irish immigrants, dug channels across vast stretches of the state—all part of an ambitious plan to move people and goods by water from Lake Erie to the Ohio River and, in the process, open the Indiana frontier to development. The plan failed badly, as plans often do. And by 1841 the state was bankrupt, leaving canals unfinished. But soon locomotives puffed across the landscape, and Hoosiers hurried to lay iron rails. Railroads meant economic growth. Hoosiers kept laying track.

Today I pore over old maps showing the dense network of railroads in Indiana, and I marvel at all the spidery lines. The state's first major railroad, the Madison and Indianapolis (M&I), was completed in 1847 and it stretched from the Ohio River to the Hoosier capital. By 1854, rail ran the length of the state, and Indiana boasted 18 railroad companies and 1,400 miles of track. That 19th-century Hoosier farmers and merchants embraced rail transportation doesn't surprise me—not with steam-powered trains hauling tons of freight at a low cost and carrying passengers quickly over great distances. What surprises—or, more specifically, impresses—me is that by the early 1900s Indiana was a leader in short-distance city-to-city rail travel. Hoosiers hopped on interurbans, electric rail cars tethered to power lines above the track, and traveled

> "In this state with the official motto 'Crossroads of America,' how will my neighbors and I move about in the future? Sure, drones will deliver our packages and computers will drive our cars. But might we see more light rail and bus-rapid transit? Electric bikes? Gyrocopters in every garage?"

from places such as Greenwood to Indianapolis to work. Or Alexandria to Anderson to shop. Or Delphi to Logansport to visit relatives. Dozens of interurban companies, operating hundreds of cars, served the majority of Indiana's counties. Only Ohio had more miles of rails under wire.

But Hoosiers, like Americans everywhere, increasingly fell in love with those newfangled horseless carriages. And Indiana wagon-makers and buggy-builders wasted no time manufacturing the gasoline-powered contraptions. By 1919, automobiles and auto parts were being produced by nearly 175 businesses throughout the state—from Kokomo to Auburn, Connersville to South Bend. Of course, Detroit, Michigan emerged as the world's auto-making capital, hastening the demise of Indiana's small car companies. Still, whether in plain-black Fords or stylish Cords, Hoosiers took to the roads with relish. And by golly, when they'd had it with rutted rural roadways, they demanded—and got—paved roads, hundreds of miles of smoothly surfaced roadbed by the mid-1920s, more than 10,000 miles by 1940.

Then came the interstates, those high-speed highways that brought me to Auburn. The stretch of I-69 from Indianapolis to the Michigan line was completed in 1971, just in time for my journey north. I still drive up and down I-69, my dependable zip-line to Indianapolis, which remains a tangle of interstates—and also home to an international airport. For many Hoosiers, myself included, transportation today often means boarding a jet plane and taking to the skies.

So I wonder: In this state with the official motto "Crossroads of America," how will my neighbors and I move about in the future? Sure, drones will deliver our packages and computers will drive our cars. But might we see more light rail and bus rapid transit? Electric bikes? Gyrocopters in every garage?

I leave such questions to others, including aerospace experts at universities such as Purdue. Future transportation, after all, may take me literally out of this world. But for now, running shoes sit by my door, and a lush greenway beckons. Muscle power, anyone? C'mon. Let's go.

Barbara Olenyik Morrow, Auburn, is the author of books for children and adults including "Those Cars of Auburn," "Hardwood Glory: A Life of John Wooden" and "Nature's Storyteller: The Life of Gene Stratton-Porter."

Rona Schwarz

The Deer's Mill covered bridge in Shades State Park transports passengers across Sugar Creek. This 275-foot Montgomery County structure was built in 1878 by J.J. Daniels. Indiana is home to nearly 100 covered bridges, with the largest number—31—in Parke County.

Indiana Voices: David Cook

David Cook is a co-founder of the Farm Heritage Trail in Thorntown. Throughout the state, abandoned railroad corridors are being transformed into rail trails for hiking, biking and horseback riding. According to the Indiana Department of Natural Resources, the state boasts more than 3,200 miles of trails, and more than 98 percent of Hoosiers live within 15 minutes of a trail.

"I grew up in Thorntown, midway between Lafayette and Indianapolis. My hometown was a stop on a railroad line originally built in the 1850s by a group of Lafayette businessmen. They envisioned transporting grain and cattle from the Indiana heartland to the Ohio and Mississippi River and ports beyond.

"In the early 1900s nearly every small town in Indiana had a railroad running through it, but by the 1970s national consolidation of the rail system was in full swing and trains no longer passed through Thorntown.

"A decade later, our railroad tracks had been removed and the rail corridor had become a weed-infested dumping ground. One day in the 1980s, a client of my law firm inquired about converting this community eyesore to a recreational trail similar to those she had seen in northern Indiana and Ohio, where her children lived. After talking to a couple of friends about the possibilities, we formed the nonprofit organization Friends of Boone County Trails, Inc.

"The plan soon became a community endeavor. A group of Purdue University Landscape Architecture students designed the trail as their senior project and coined the name 'Farm Heritage Trail.' The Indiana Department of Natural Resources provided matching grants totaling $1 million to create the 10 miles of trail between Thorntown and Lebanon.

"Historically, this same transportation corridor was on the path of the Lincoln inaugural and funeral trains in 1860 and 1865. Today, the former railroad tracks have been transformed into a trail where hikers and bikers can enjoy fresh air along with vistas of farm fields and wildlife, free of motor vehicles.

"Hoosiers have always been on the move by one mode of transportation or another, and it has been a unique opportunity for me to help preserve and transform this historic and healthy transportation corridor."

John Whalen

David Cook takes a ride on the Farm Heritage Trail.

Steve Blackwell

Bike-share programs now provide a convenient and environmentally sound form of hop-on, hop-off transportation in several Indiana cities, including Indianapolis (pictured here) and Carmel.

President Lincoln's funeral train car arrives in the Jennings County town of Vernon on April 26, 2015. During the month of the 150th anniversary of Lincoln's assassination, the train re-created the journey of the funeral train throughout the East and Midwest.

Small railroad depots like this one dotted the Indiana landscape in the 19th century as the railroad network expanded throughout the state. This Nappanee depot (note the misspelling of the town's name on the sign) was built in 1874, when the Baltimore & Ohio Railroad started service in the area. It was destroyed by fire in 1985 after being moved and repurposed.

Indiana Voices: Andrew Beckman

Andrew Beckman is archivist at the Studebaker National Museum in South Bend.

Matt Cashore, Studebaker National Museum

"Essentially, the American automobile industry started in Indiana, Michigan and Ohio. In the early age of automobiles, Indiana was producing some of the finest cars in the nation. Not many people know that.

"Indiana had its share of solid engineers who knew how to put their ideas into motion. Haynes Automobile Company of Kokomo claims the title of the nation's first automobile manufacturer.

"Look at what the Duesenberg Brothers brought to the table: The first hydraulic brakes were on their 1921 Model A. The Auburn Company's front-wheel drive Cord L29, built in the late 1920s, foreshadowed the industry's front-wheel drive renaissance in the 1970s and 1980s. The technological excellence of the Marmon and Stutz companies also was unparalleled.

"Studebaker was the world's largest transportation manufacturer in the horse-drawn era, and it was located right here in South Bend. No one was bigger: Studebaker was the General Motors of the wagon-making industry. By the 1880s they were billing themselves as the world's largest builder of buggies and wagons. After the Depression, Studebaker was the last soldier left in Indiana's auto-manufacturing industry.

"Many, many Hoosiers put their talents into building some of the world's finest automobiles."

Lisa Conrad

This Auburn Beauty-Six automobile, introduced in 1919, was on display at the Auburn-Duesenberg Classic Car Show and Festival, held each year the week before Labor Day in its namesake town.

The historic Wabash and Erie Canal, though no longer used as a major transportation route, still carries travelers. When completed in 1853 it was the nation's longest canal, stretching 468 miles from Toledo, Ohio to Evansville. Its completion meant that, through a series of connected waterways, boats could travel from New York City to New Orleans. Today The Delphi, a replica of a 19th-century canal boat, transports visitors at the Wabash & Erie Canal museum in Carroll County.

Victoria Seest

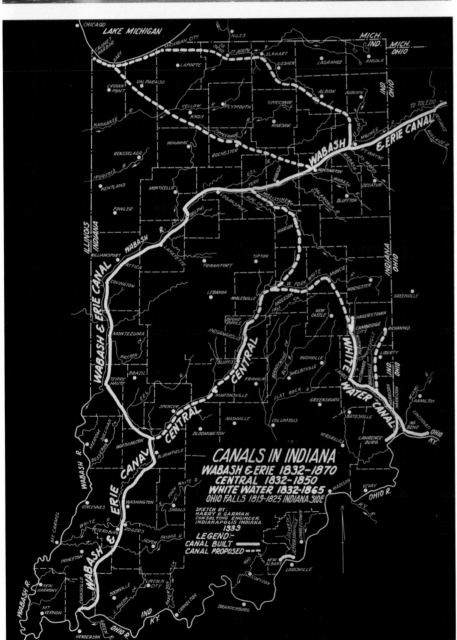

This 1939 map highlights Indiana's state-wide reach of canals. In addition to the 472 miles of canals that were built, another 385 miles were proposed.

Harry O. Garman, Indiana Historical Society

Indiana Voices: Rich Cooper

Jeff LeFors

The Port of Indiana, Burns Harbor, Porter County

Indiana's waterways have played a major role in Indiana's history and continue to play a significant role in the state's economy. The Ports of Indiana, founded in 1961, is a statewide port authority operating a port on Lake Michigan and two on the Ohio River. These ports provide the state with thousands of acres of maritime industrial parks that enable companies to connect to international markets via ships, barges, railroads and highways. Port companies regularly ship cargo to or from 28 countries and 47 states.

"Indiana has a rich and prosperous history in maritime shipping. From launching the Lewis & Clark Expedition on the Ohio River in 1803 to receiving the state's first ocean vessels on Lake Michigan in the 1970s, Indiana has leveraged its unique waterways to grow its economy and access to the world.

"Indiana's border is 57 percent water, and we generally rank in the top 10 states for domestic waterborne shipments and in the top 15 when you include international shipments.

"Few states can claim access to two of the busiest inland waterways in the world: the Ohio-Mississippi rivers and the Great Lakes. And no other state can combine this access with a location at the midpoint of the U.S. population and a statewide port authority operating multiple ports on two waterways.

"Why is waterborne shipping important? It accounts for 90 percent of world trade. Rivers, lakes and oceans provide efficient corridors for cargo movements. One towboat moving 15 river barges can haul more grain than 1,000 trucks—and one Great Lakes vessel carries more iron ore than 2,300 trucks. Maritime shipping is the safest, most environmentally friendly and economical mode of transportation."

~ *Rich Cooper, CEO, Ports of Indiana*

William J. Lackner

A coal barge approaches the Milton-Madison bridge on the Ohio River. By 1850, the southern Indiana city of Newburgh was one of the largest riverports on the Ohio-Mississippi Rivers between Cincinnati and New Orleans, in large part due to coal mining.

INFact

Indiana's Public Ports

- *Provide direct waterway access to two U.S. coasts*
- *Handle 4,000 barges per year on the Ohio River and Lake Michigan*
- *Handle 150 ocean and lake vessels per year on Lake Michigan*
- *Contribute more than $6 billion per year to the state's economy and support over 50,000 jobs*
- *Ship coal, grain, steel, fertilizer, limestone, ethanol, road salt, minerals, heavy equipment as well as many other dry, liquid and specialty project cargoes*
- *Exceeded 10 million tons of shipments in one year for the first time in 2014*

Source: Ports of Indiana

James A. Strain

Built in 1904 to help boaters find their way safely to harbor, the Michigan City lighthouse is today the only public operating lighthouse in Indiana. The city's first lighthouse, built in 1858, is now a tourist attraction in Millennium Park.

An early-morning shot from the interior of Williams Bridge in Lawrence County. Built in 1884, this 376-foot covered bridge spans the East Fork of the White River.

The Tulip Trestle, also known as the Greene County Viaduct, was built in 1906 near Bloomfield. One of the longest of this type in the world, it stretches nearly half a mile over the fields below and is still in use today.

This crumbling Fort Wayne bridge is a relic from the first third of the 20th century, when electric-powered interurban trains were the major mode of transportation between Indiana towns. The term "interurban" was likely coined by U.S. Congressman and State Sen. Charles L. Henry of Anderson. In its heyday, the Indianapolis Traction Terminal was the largest interurban station in the world, through which 7 million passengers passed each year.
Daniel A. Baker

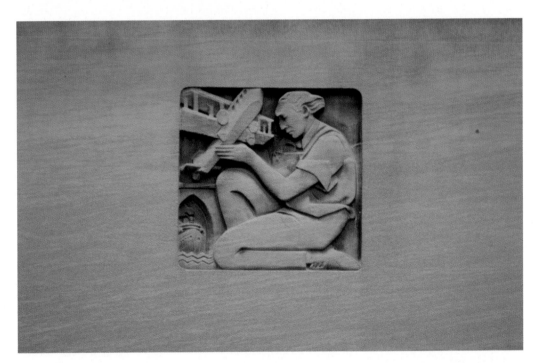

A limestone carving on the façade of the Indiana State Library in downtown Indianapolis.
John Whalen

The Madison Society

An early interurban in Jefferson County.

Indiana State Library Collection

In the early part of the 20th century, buggies and interurbans competed for space on Washington Street in downtown Indianapolis. Washington Street is a section of the National Road.

JJ Canull

Horse-drawn buggies remain the preferred mode of transport in Indiana's Amish community.

Judi Barr

This 1874 bridge, one of the oldest iron bridges in Indiana, was originally built near Camden. It has found new life as a pedestrian bridge over the Wabash & Erie Canal as part of the Delphi Historical Trails.

The newest stretch of interstate highway in the state is the 112-mile section of I-69 that runs from north of Odon to the south side of Evansville. It's the first major Indiana section completed of the planned national extension of I-69 southwest from Indianapolis to Texas.

Indiana Department of Transportation

101

The first attempt at an official airmail flight in the United States, carrying 123 letters and 23 pamphlets, launched from Lafayette on Aug. 17, 1859. The air balloon Jupiter, piloted by Professor John Wise, was headed for New York but flew off course and settled near Crawfordsville, a mere 30 miles away—prompting the Lafayette Daily Courier to wisecrack that the flight was "trans-county-nental." The postmarked letters were dispatched by train to New York for delivery. One of those letters resides today at the Smithsonian National Postal Museum in Washington, D.C.

The Gary Aquatorium, a 1920s beach bathhouse designated a National Historic Landmark, is home to a memorial to Octave Chanute, the father of flight. In the summer of 1896 Chanute, a mentor to the Wright Brothers, partnered with others to launch hang gliders from the Miller Beach lakeshore dunes.

The famed aviator Wilbur Wright was born in this Millville farmhouse in 1867; he attended high school in Richmond. The house is now part of the Wilbur Wright Birthplace and Museum.

Indianapolis International Airport, the largest airport in Indiana, with an average of 140 flights each day, serves more than 7.4 million passengers annually and is the world's 22nd largest cargo facility. It was named the best airport in North America by Airports International Council in 2010, 2012, 2013 and 2014, based on a survey of air travelers.

The Cutting Edge

Unmanned aerial systems, commonly known as drones, are on the cutting edge of transportation. Indiana State is the first university in the state to receive authorization from the Federal Aviation Administration to operate these systems. The authorization covers Terre Haute International Airport-Hulman Field and the Indiana National Guard's Muscatatuck Urban Training Center. Indiana State offers a minor in unmanned systems and has plans to offer a bachelor's degree in the subject.

Donald J. Bonte Jr., Director of ISU's Center for Unmanned Systems Research and Human Capital Development, says, "Our unmanned systems program at Indiana State focuses on non-conflict uses of the technology, such as natural disaster response, humanitarian relief, environmental assessments and precision agriculture."

An aerial view of the National Guard's Muscatatuck Urban Training Center.

Indiana State University has been authorized to fly this unmanned vehicle called the Draganflyer.

By John Thompson

When I moved to Indiana 31 years ago, I immediately began to appreciate the richness of innovation and business prowess of my new home. I was fortunate to relocate to Indiana to lead Mays Chemical Company's sales effort, which took me across Indiana, the United States and the Americas. In this role, I could compare the richness of Indiana's business environment to all of the Americas. Ahhh … as a young man in my late 20s, what did I see?

I saw Eli Lilly and Co., which for more than 100 years had been improving the lives of people and animals by producing amazing products in Tippecanoe, Clinton, Hancock and Marion counties.

And who would have thought that a young J. Irwin Miller would found one of the architectural capitals of America in Bartholomew County on the strength of an industrial powerhouse: Cummins Engine. Today Cummins' diesel- and gas-powered engines are the most fuel-efficient and sought-after in the world. This global producer, with 54,000 employees operating on every continent, chooses to continue its commitment to the Hoosier state with its new research and development center in Seymour and its distribution division headquarters in Indianapolis.

We continue our rich automotive production history with Chrysler and Delphi in Kokomo, Toyota in Princeton, GM in Fort Wayne, Allison Transmission in Indianapolis, Subaru of Indiana Automotive, Inc. in Lafayette and AM

continued

General in Mishawaka. We find Jasper Engines & Transmissions, Dallara, NTN Driveshaft, Magna Powertrain, Remy and Stant operating throughout Indiana. We are an automotive juggernaut!

Tom Easterday of Subaru of Indiana had this to say: "Indiana's automotive heritage and aggressive efforts to attract international automakers and automotive suppliers have paid substantial dividends for our state. Indiana has also served as a model for other states in welcoming Japanese investment and extending Hoosier hospitality to those Japanese who have come to Indiana for business reasons—many of whom now call Indiana their home.

"Subaru of Indiana Automotive (SIA) and our many suppliers across Indiana have clearly benefited from our state's highly skilled workforce, favorable tax/regulatory environment, extensive interstate highway system, cooperation between local and state governments and the outstanding technology, engineering and business schools at Indiana's colleges and universities. SIA has exported Subaru vehicles to more than 50 countries around the world; and since sales of the SIA-built Subaru Legacy and Outback have grown substantially in the U.S. market in recent years, SIA and several of our Indiana-based suppliers have expanded. SIA's success is a result of the excellent teamwork, strong work ethic and commitment to quality of our Hoosier workforce."

> "Given the emphasis placed on family by Hoosiers, the number of multigenerational family businesses is no surprise."

Steel continues to be at the core of the auto industry and many others, including construction, heavy equipment, medical products and appliances. Innovation in steel production has flourished across the state, ranging from our historical Lake County base with U.S. Steel and Arcelor Mittal, to Fort Wayne-based Steel Dynamics with its operations in Clark and DeKalb counties, to Nucor in Montgomery County.

Indiana is well-known and respected for its creativity in medical products, with Kosciusko County—the world epicenter for orthopedics development and manufacturing—as a highlight. Biomet, Zimmer and the DePuy Synthes Companies of Johnson & Johnson form the basis for this orthopedic cluster, with $11 billion in revenue and more than 13,000 employees, representing 45 percent of the jobs in Kosciusko County. Bloomington is the home of the billion-dollar, privately owned Cook Group, producing 16,000 medical devices and products and employing more than 9,000.

Given the emphasis placed on family by Hoosiers, the number of multigenerational family businesses is no surprise. LDI, Ltd. in Indianapolis has sales exceeding $1 billion and thousands of employees around the globe. There's Reilly Industries, based in Indianapolis and now owned by Vertellus; Jayco in Middlebury, with 47 years of RV production; and Calumet Specialty Products Partners, specializing in oil refining, environmental remediation and materials.

Koch Enterprises, which began as a tin shop in Indianapolis, is now a distribution and auto parts manufacturing company based in Evansville. "The favorable business climate in Indiana and great team members have enabled our family manufacturing and wholesale distribution businesses to expand and prosper for more than 140 years. Through organic growth and acquisitions, and now led by the fifth generation, our sales exceed $1 billion," said company chairman Robert L. Koch II.

Employee-owned companies like Herff Jones in Indianapolis and Rea Magnet Wire in Fort Wayne provide an opportunity for employees to share directly in wealth creation. For example, Herff Jones employees, as shareholders, were richly rewarded when the company was purchased by management and a private-equity partner. It's wonderful to see the employees share in the bounty of their skilled and hard work.

Our technology parks are the centers of innovation today: places like Discovery Park in Lafayette, Flagship Enterprise

Vincent Walter

Purdue University's Discovery Park

Center in Anderson, Purdue Technology Center in Crown Point and Mid-America Science Park in Scottsburg. Innovation and Ignition parks in South Bend continue the legacy of Indiana's creativity in manufacturing and business services development. Successful startups born in Innovation Park move on to Ignition Park, continuing to receive support services as they grow.

Ignition Park, built on the grounds of the former Studebaker auto plant, is the site of a $36 million public-private partnership to develop a Turbomachinery Research Facility for the development of gas turbine engines used in commercial and military aircraft, power plants and the oil and gas industry. Notre Dame, GE, the city of South Bend, Great Lakes Capital, the Indiana Economic Development Corporation and Indiana Michigan Power are involved in the effort. It's like weaving a blanket of interconnectedness across our great state, with GE also investing $10 million in advanced manufacturing research at Purdue to lower cost, improve speed and drive innovation in tomorrow's factories. At the same time, GE invested $115 million in a new LEAP jet engine facility in West Lafayette.

Our universities and state and local governments, along with a well-educated, highly trained workforce, come together in a business-friendly environment to attract the best global companies and to advance technology, producing leading-edge products and services for tomorrow. Ahhh … I love this state of mine.

Angie's List, Interactive Intelligence, Apparatus, Compendium, Endocyte, Aprimo, ChaCha, Nico and Baker Hill are companies that speak to the creativity of our entrepreneurs. They have drawn rapidly growing interest from the venture capital community across the country, including firms like Centerfield Capital Partners; Lynx Capital; Allos Ventures; Hammond Kennedy, Whitney & Company; Battery Ventures and Spring Mill Venture Partners.

Halo Group and other angel investors are providing earlier-stage capital to grow our businesses. These investors are attracted by the growing list of Hoosier companies that have started, grown up and been sold, generating high returns for investors who saw the promise of ExactTarget, Marcadia, Suros Surgical, Emerging Threats Pro and other success stories. The state does its part to encourage such activity through the Indiana Economic Development Corporation and Elevate Ventures, which manages the flow of state and federal venture dollars.

It's refreshing to enjoy the growth of women- and minority-owned businesses from the Ohio River to Lake Michigan, with Fort Wayne-based Vera Bradley, Indianapolis-based Angie's List and Langham Logistics all including one or more women among its founders. Mays Chemical, Harris and Ford in Indianapolis, Telamon in Carmel, and Powers and Sons in Gary are all minority-owned businesses of size and scale, home-grown right here in Indiana. The thousands of jobs created by these businesses, accompanied by tens of millions of dollars of capital investment, speak to the importance of an inclusive approach to creating jobs and increasing economic activity.

As a young man traveling from Indianapolis to Mishawaka to meet with AM General, to Clinton to visit Eli Lilly and Co., or to NSWC Crane in Martin County, I developed an excitement for the work ethic and talent of Hoosiers. This is a phenomenal state that has contributed greatly to America and to the world in so many ways, none greater than business. However, the best is yet to come.

John Thompson is an Indianapolis-based business consultant and the chairman and CEO of four Indianapolis companies: Thompson Distribution Co. Inc.; First Electric Supply Co. LLC; the architectural and engineering design firm CMID; and BC-SESCO, a fabricator and installer of millwork.

Indiana Voices: Nick Davidson

Nick Davidson

Nick Davidson and his family own Tin Man Brewing in Evansville.

"Evansville, my hometown, has a deep history in brewing stretching all the way back to the 1830s. Evansville's first brewery, Old Brewery, opened in 1837 and after more than 100 years of changing hands and merging with other breweries became the Sterling Brewery. I remember Sterling from my childhood and passed by the brewery almost every day. Unfortunately, in 1997, the year I graduated from high school, the brewery closed and the next year it was torn down. That coincidentally was the year I started home-brewing.

"My obsession with the beer-making process all started when I moved away from Evansville to attend college in Chicago. After college, I moved to Indianapolis and opened my first business. During this time I witnessed the craft beer culture really take off in Indy. When I sold my business in 2009, I moved back to my hometown of Evansville and decided that I wanted to help bring that craft beer movement to the place where I grew up. I took my love of home-brewing, which I had been doing since my college days, and opened Tin Man Brewing Co. in 2012."

Jordan Barclay

John Whalen

A Saturday afternoon at 18th Street Brewery in Gary

❚NFact

Brewing Comes Full Circle

The history of beer breweries in Indiana dates back to 1816, when there were two. The number peaked at 66 in 1880 before a long descent—hastened by Prohibition—that took the number back to two by 1975. A resurgence that started about 10 years ago makes today the golden age of brewing in Indiana.

1975 - 2	2005 - 21
1990 - 4	2010 - 34
1995 - 7	2014 – 103
2000 - 21	

Source: Bob Ostrander, indianabeer.com

The Derrick Morris Collection

108

Madam C.J. Walker, top, and ExactTarget founder Scott Dorsey, below, are entrepreneurs from different centuries. Walker, once the nation's wealthiest black woman, moved her beauty products company from Denver to Indianapolis in 1910 for access to the city's freight routes. Dorsey, shown below on Monument Circle with employees of ExactTarget, co-founded the email and digital marketing firm in Indianapolis in 2000.

Indiana Voices: Chris Hall

Chris Hall is communications director for Velocity Indiana, a business accelerator, a co-working space and source of education for future Hoosier entrepreneurs. It operates from a building in downtown Jeffersonville that was once used to outfit the interiors of passenger rail cars. Business accelerators, which have become an industry unto themselves, have sprung up across the state to help entrepreneurs turn their ideas into the companies of tomorrow.

"My startup business failed just months after going through Velocity's inaugural accelerator program. Failing is not a pleasant experience, but it happens when you discover that your original assumptions were flawed after six months of planning and eight months of execution. Velocity pushed me over a 100-day period to rapidly determine the viability of my business. The answer at the end of the rainbow wasn't what I had planned or hoped for, but that's not what mattered. Process mattered.

"After falling short, I was recruited to be a part of building Velocity into a hub of entrepreneurial activity. The idea of a place where people can push themselves, fall short and achieve, together, is important. I graciously accepted.

"The people we work with here have had a big impact on Jeffersonville and its southern Indiana neighbors. Sixteen local startups have come through Velocity's accelerator program and 13 of them are still operating and growing today. Hundreds of kids have been introduced to coding here and are asking for new classes faster than curriculum can be built. And dozens of fledgling businesses have worked in Velocity's coworking and office space. Some have moved on. The rest are moving forward. We're all still pushing."

Chris Hall

Chris Hall and his son, Cassius, take a break at Velocity after whiteboarding a video game concept Cassius came up with. Says Hall, "We wore ties because it was an official business meeting and Cassius knew it was important."

Kimball International, a Jasper company that makes furniture for the office and hospitality sectors, has its roots in the manufacturing of wood furniture, such as cabinets and pianos. Indiana's hardwoods industry generates a statewide economic impact of more than $16 billion. The state's hardwood products—worth $8 billion in 2010—include kitchen cabinets, caskets, manufactured homes, plywood products and furniture.

Denise Szocka,
Indiana Department
of Environmental Management

Rich Vorhees

Fiberglass Freaks in Logansport is licensed by DC Comics to build and sell full-scale, drivable replicas of the 1966 Batmobile, made popular in the Batman comic strip and 1960s television show. It takes the company's 17 artisans about six months to build one of the handcrafted cars.

The iconic Coca-Cola bottle was designed in 1915 in Terre Haute by Earl R. Dean, foreman and bottle designer for The Root Glass Co.
Vigo County Historical Society

Indiana Voices: Jean Ann Harcourt

Jean Ann Harcourt is president of Harcourt Outlines, the pencil and school supplies company founded by her mom, dad and grandpa in the tiny Rush County town of Milroy.

"Harcourt Outlines was started in 1956 in an old chicken house with a dirt floor. My brother and business partner, Joe Harcourt, now the vice president of sales and marketing, was 5 years old and I was 3. Our parents, Conrad C. and Norma S. Harcourt, along with our grandpa, Pick Harcourt, started printing outline maps on carbon master units for use on duplicating machines. They sold school name pencils as a secondary line.

"The demand for printed master units fell off with the invention of copy machines, but the sale of school name pencils continued to grow. In 1958, Grandpa Pick invented and perfected a pencil vending machine to be loaned free to schools if the schools continued to buy our pencils. We still have 24,000 vending machines located in 11,000 schools across the USA.

Harcourt Outlines
Jean Ann Harcourt and her brother, Joe Harcourt, are the third-generation owners of Harcourt Outlines. Their pencil vending machines are found in schools across the country.

"Our dad died unexpectedly of a heart attack in 1975 when he was just 48. Joe was 24 years old and I was 22, with a brand new college diploma in business administration ... we were IN CHARGE! The past 39 years have been interesting, with many good years and several stressful ones thanks to all the changes in technology. Students use iPads today and not many pencils.

"Harcourt Outlines continues to adapt. Today we offer student planners, fundraising programs, motivational products and back-to-school packs."

Indiana Voices: Gustavo Rodriguez

Gustavo Rodriguez owns and operates Caliente Cuban Café with his wife, Yalili Mesa, in the East State Village area of Fort Wayne.

"We arrived here from Cuba in June of 2000 as political refugees. Yalili was in the computer field in Cuba, and in the United States she worked as an operator in sewing factories. The economic crisis of 2008 pushed her to consider her career options. A friend suggested Yalili start a business. It was not until she signed a lease that she envisioned a sandwich shop. Neither of us had ever owned or operated a business when Yalili opened Caliente by herself in early 2009. I quit my job in July of the same year and joined her because operating the sandwich shop was practically impossible for only one person.

"Our son, Nestor, now 22, studied at Purdue and is about to graduate as a Marine. He has worked in the restaurant since he was 17. Now our youngest son, Bryan, who is in 7th grade, will experience his first summer as an 'assistant' in the restaurant.

Julio N. Garcia
Gustavo Rodriguez and his wife, Yalili Mesa, in their Fort Wayne sandwich shop, Caliente Cuban Cafe.

"Our restaurant offers a unique experience connecting people with food, language and culture. The people in Fort Wayne like to eat, and we like cooking. It is the perfect combination."

The Fashion Mall in Indianapolis is owned by Simon Property Group, the largest owner of retail properties in the United States.

This family-owned general store in Rush County, circa 1905, recalls a time when many Hoosiers knew their local merchant. Many of today's consumers shop at big-box stores and large retail centers. By early 2015, 7 percent of all U.S. retail transactions occurred online.

Started in Indianapolis by serial tech entrepreneur Scott Jones, Lemonade Day teaches kids how to start, own and operate their own business: a lemonade stand. The aim is to inspire the next generation of Hoosier entrepreneurs. More than 50,000 kids in central Indiana have participated since the first Lemonade Day in 2010.

Cummins Inc., based in Columbus, designs, manufactures, sells and services diesel engines and related technology around the world.
Indianapolis Business Journal

Elkhart County Convention and Visitors Bureau

Elkhart County is the hub of recreational vehicle manufacturing in the United States. Approximately 83 percent of domestic RV manufacturing occurs in Elkhart and adjacent LaGrange County.

Allison Transmission

Founded by James Allison in 1915, Allison Transmission is the world's largest manufacturer of commercial-duty automatic transmissions and hybrid propulsion systems.

▮NFact

Indiana's Biggest Industries

Measured by gross domestic product, the dollar values of Indiana's largest industry sectors are:

- Manufacturing ($95.3 billion)
- Finance, insurance, real estate, rental, and leasing ($46 billion)
- Government ($28.8 billion)
- Educational services, health care and social assistance ($27.5 billion)
- Professional & business services ($25.3 billion)

Source: Indiana Business Research Center, Kelley School of Business, Indiana University

The Cord, which started production in 1929 in Auburn, was one of many luxury cars made in Indiana in the first half of the 20th century before most domestic manufacturing migrated to Detroit.

James Eickman

Studebaker Corp.'s administration building, shown in about 1915, is representative of the auto industry and the jobs it created for South Bend and other cities and towns that relied heavily on manufacturing. Studebaker's South Bend factories sat idle for years after the last Avanti rolled off the line in 1963, but the buildings have been repurposed into research labs and business incubators.

Studebaker National Museum

Subaru of Indiana Automotive Inc., located in Lafayette, is among the newest wave of auto manufacturers to call Indiana home. Toyota (Princeton) and Honda (Greensburg) are the other big Japanese brands that have operations in the state. Among domestic producers, General Motors opened a huge plant in Fort Wayne in 1986 that continues to grow.

Indianapolis Business Journal

Brands with Indiana Roots

Wick's Pies

Wick's Pies, based in Winchester in Randolph County, sells its desserts in 25 of the 50 states.

Ken Kosky

Orville Redenbacher, a native of Brazil in Clay County, was an agricultural scientist whose hybrid popcorn became one of the country's most famous brands. This likeness of him is from the Porter County Popcorn Festival.

Red Gold, based in Elwood, has been producing tomato products since 1942.

Lesley Ackman

Clabber Girl Baking Powder, one of America's most famous brands, is headquartered in Terre Haute.

The famous Ball home-canning jar came from Muncie, where the Ball brothers moved their business in 1887 to take advantage of the area's abundant natural gas reserves, which are used in the manufacturing of glass.

Dr. William M. Scholl, a native of La Porte, is the namesake and founder of "Dr. Scholl's," a brand of footwear and foot-care products.

The discovery of natural gas sparked the growth of Howard County's rich glass heritage. The world's oldest manufacturer of opalescent and cathedral stained glass, Kokomo Opalescent Glass has been in operation since 1888. KOG produced much of the glass used by Louis Comfort Tiffany in his New York studios.

Indiana Voices: Joseph Pete

"The Ottoman Empire drafted my great-grandfather, who then fled from Macedonia to the United States. After landing at Ellis Island, he heard opportunity awaited in Gary, which U.S. Steel had just transformed from frigid marshland off Lake Michigan to a bustling company town that drew immigrants from the world over. He ended up toiling in the sprawling Gary Works, then the largest steel mill anywhere.

"His son, my grandfather, showed an aptitude for drawing in school so they pushed him to become an architectural draftsman at the mill. He worked on projects such as the Sears Tower, the John Hancock Center, the St. Louis Arch, and the Houston Astrodome. Northwest Indiana's steel industry built up much of 20th century America. You can still find Calumet Region steel in almost any appliance or car on the road.

"Now I cover the local steel business as a newspaper reporter. Some say the mills are a husk of what they were, with a fraction of the workforce. But they remain Northwest Indiana's second-largest employer and are still vital economically. Lake and Porter Counties have led the nation in steelmaking for more than 30 years, and together crank out more steel than any state."

Jonathan Miano

Joseph Pete, right, conducts interviews for a story at one of the northwest Indiana steel facilities he writes about for The Times of Northwest Indiana.

Steel mills in Michigan City

Marsha Williamson Mohr

Fog

...hot wild core of the earth, heavier than
we can even imagine.
D.H. Lawrence, "Underneath"

From cold winds
that bring signals
through our factory walls,

to the high dunes
where you can stand and see Chicago
shimmer on the rim of a great lake,

where market-clatter and jazz
is silent in the marram;

from Saulk Trails,
where all those stories and dreams
that have died since the Potawatami
can be heard in a muffled wave,

you can still hear through the warm fog of our land

mills ladle a hot core
of nickel,

and bone.

~ William Buckley

John Whalen

Kids play on a Lake Michigan beach, with the city of Gary in the background.

119

By Paul Helmke

Early in my undergraduate years at Indiana University, I was told that Indiana never wanted to be one of the first states to try something, and never one of the last. This frustrated me—if the idea was good, why shouldn't we be one of the first to implement it?

Over 60 years of exposure to Indiana politics has given me some insight into what works and doesn't work with our government. Whenever changes are proposed to make local or state government more efficient, however, the prevailing attitude is usually not just "if it ain't broke, don't fix it," but "let's wait until it's broke, falling completely apart and rusting, and then maybe we'll look at it."

We have a lot more government than most Hoosiers realize. At the start, the structure made sense. Everyone lived in the state, a county and a township. From 15 counties in 1816, we now have 92 counties (and more than 1,000 townships).

The township was the main contact point for individuals needing something from government. Townships were small enough to handle daily issues. They were in charge of public education and had a one-room schoolhouse in the center of the township so all the children could walk there and back. The schoolhouse bell could be heard by most of the people in the township and summoned volunteers who could respond to fight fires or deal with other emergencies. The township could then deal with "poor relief" and help provide public assistance to folks impacted by these emergencies.

continued

Stained glass domed ceiling of the Indiana State Capitol
Rona Schwarz

County government dealt with the weekly or monthly issues that might require a buggy ride to the centrally located county courthouse. Here, you could file a lawsuit, probate a will, record a deed, pay property taxes, and take care of issues impacting land, property and official records. The county sheriff arrested lawbreakers and put them in the county jail. The three-person board of county commissioners would meet monthly to handle road, bridge and drainage issues benefitting the dispersed farmers and tradesmen, and set the property-tax rates to pay for these services.

The state had a much smaller role in Hoosier lives. Major infrastructure projects, state militia service and some provision for higher education pretty much filled the slim agenda for the state government. The original Indiana Constitution of 1816 was replaced just once, in 1851, primarily to put limits on borrowing by government after the canal industry collapsed and the state went bankrupt.

For people who chose to live close to each other, the state allowed the creation of towns and cities. The public safety and infrastructure challenges of these more densely populated spaces meant more governmental responsibility and authority in the hands of the town and city councils, clerks, mayors and local officials. After all, if your neighbor leaves garbage out or has a home that is a fire hazard, this impacts you a lot more when you live close together in the city than when you're miles apart in the country.

"In politics, southern Indiana has reflected its ties to the South with conservatism and traditional Democratic sympathies. Northern Indiana politics reflect the ethnic and racial migrations of the last 200 years."

There is a lot of overlap in this structure. I used to give speeches where I'd ask the listeners if they lived in the city or in the county. I'd get a lot of split crowds until I pointed out that everyone who lived in the city also lived in the county. The fact that taxes were owed to all of these government units, plus the school district and a myriad of service districts, confused people even more.

Over time, we dealt with many of these overlaps and confusions. School districts were formed from consolidations of township and city schools. County small claims courts replaced the township-based "justices of the peace." Township fire departments and "poor relief" functions play a lot smaller role than in the past. Township assessors, when they still exist, have to follow strict "equalization" formulas.

The biggest example of change for county—and city—government came at the end of 1960s when then-Mayor Richard Lugar convinced the Legislature to expand Indianapolis' boundaries to the Marion County lines and combined many governmental functions under "Unigov." This greatly increased the clout of what had been known as "Naptown" and helped set the stage for the growing capital city of today.

Permissive annexation laws helped cities like Fort Wayne grow from about 170,000 when I became mayor in 1987 to nearly 260,000 in 2016, but unhappy suburbanites in Allen County, as well as in other counties with growing cities like Carmel, helped pressure their legislators to move toward allowing annexation only when the residents consented.

Despite these changes, we still elect more than 1,000 township trustees and 3,000 township advisory board members; more than 270 county commissioners, 460 county council members and 500 other county department officers; more than 100 mayors and city clerks and 800 city council members; as well as more than 2,000 town board members. This does not include elected judges, prosecutors or school board members. It does not include state or federal officials elected from Indiana.

We have strengthened state government over the years. Governors have had greater control since the 1930s (thanks to Paul McNutt) and have been able to run for two consecutive terms since the early 1970s (and Otis Bowen, Robert Orr, Evan Bayh, Frank O'Bannon and Mitch Daniels all have shown that voters like this option). The Legislature now meets every year rather than every other year. The extra "short" session established in the early 1970s was supposed to be for emergency financial issues, but now seems to be pretty all-inclusive in its reach. We still elect a lot of other statewide officials, even some who have had their power limited by the Legislature.

For a long time, I had trouble reconciling Hoosier mistrust of government with all of these elected officials and overlapping jurisdictions, but two reasons for our current system now seem clear to me: First, the more people we elect and the more competing units we create, the less likely any of them are ever going to be able to make big changes quickly on their own—after all, we don't want to be one of the first to try something new. Second, while most people are shocked by how we structure government, I point out that there are really "only" two groups who oppose change—Republicans and Democrats.

Yes, both major political parties have had a lot of success at all levels of Indiana government, and they don't trust changing the playing field. In politics, southern Indiana has reflected its ties to the South with conservatism and traditional Democratic sympathies. Northern Indiana politics reflect the ethnic and racial migrations of the last 200 years. Both parties have potential voters in all of these areas. For 60 years after the Civil War, Indiana contributed many politicians to the national party tickets, with Sen. Benjamin Harrison elected president in 1888. The parties frequently switch control of the governor and U.S. Senate offices, and the Democrats even carry the state for president on occasion.

Despite the resistance to change—or maybe because of it—Indiana has usually figured out how to make government reflect the will of the people for 200 years—and hopefully many more.

Paul Helmke, former president and CEO of the Brady Center/Brady Campaign to Prevent Gun Violence and three-term mayor of Fort Wayne, is a professor of practice at the Indiana University School of Public and Environmental Affairs and the founding director of the Civic Leaders Living-Learning Center. While mayor of Fort Wayne, he served as president of the U.S. Conference of Mayors.

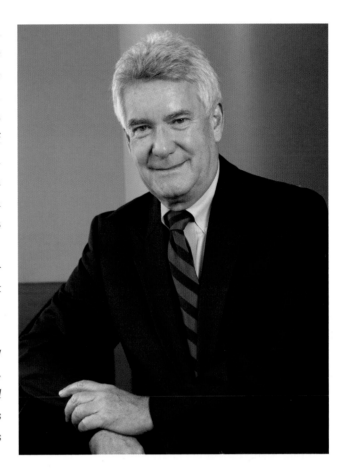

The Ohio County Courthouse in Rising Sun, built in 1845, is the oldest continuously used courthouse in the state.
René Stanley,
Indiana Bicentennial Commission

Indiana Voices: Olivia Abner

As a 10-year-old student at Morgan Elementary School in Palmyra, Olivia Abner wrote the winning essay for the 2014 Statehood Day essay contest with her entry, "History is Not Just the Past—It's Today."

"'Bicentennial moments' surround me. Growing up in Harrison County, home to Corydon and the first state capitol, I see history every day. The entire town of Corydon is historical and then there are treasures from the early years that still exist. First there is the First State Capitol itself. Then there is the Constitution Elm and stories from the people who helped to build the state of Indiana.

"The story starts in 1814, two hundred years ago this year, when a two-story limestone building was built. This building only cost three thousand dollars! It was built to serve as our first state capitol. It stands in our downtown square for all to see and learn from. I get excited when I see school buses from far-away places coming to tour Corydon. It makes me proud. After all, I've spent my whole life fifteen miles away!

"The other amazing historical monument was not built. It grew. The Constitution Elm tree was just a tree until a hot June day in 1816 when forty-three delegates came to the newly constructed State Capitol to draft our state's constitution, and it was too hot to work inside. So they went to the shade of the biggest tree around, a tree which is now called the Constitution Elm. The elm had a one hundred thirty two foot span from the tip to tip of its branches and it stood fifty feet tall. Our fore-fathers wrote the constitution under this tree from June 10th to the 29th, 1816. The tree died in 1925, but now its trunk is surrounded by beautiful cases to preserve it.

"These historical trea-sures, while old, are like time travelers coming to tell me their stories. That's why it's not just the past. It's today."

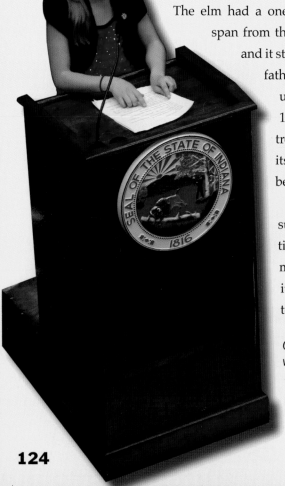

Olivia Abner reads her prize-winning essay at the Indiana Statehouse.
René Stanley, Indiana Bicentennial Commission

Alan Stewart

The first state capitol building in Corydon. Corydon became capital of the Indiana Territory in 1813 and remained the state capital until 1825.

Felicia Batman

A statue in Corydon commemorates Indiana Gov. Frank O'Bannon. O'Bannon, a native of Corydon, was 47th governor of Indiana from 1997 until his death in 2003.

State Capitol Building in Indianapolis

The Indiana Senate in session

Indiana Voices: Evan Bayh

Evan Bayh served as Indiana secretary of state from 1986-1988 before being elected 46th governor of Indiana. After serving two terms as governor, from 1989-1997, Bayh was elected to the U.S. Senate, where he served from 1999-2011.

Indiana State Archives

"I am the fourth generation of my family born in Indiana. We have historically been centered in Vigo, Owen and Putnam Counties. That makes Indiana 'home' to me in a geographic sense. My sons were born in Marion County, where my wife and I have lived for more than 30 years. But what makes Indiana home to me isn't just geography or an accident of birth. The state represents a set of values I hold dear: respect for the past, a willingness to build for the future, love of family, faith in God, devotion to country. These things make someone a Hoosier, including me.

"Indiana has continued to evolve throughout my lifetime. The state is more urban than it was in 1955 when I was born. Our economy has continued to change, transitioning from agriculture to manufacturing to service businesses to globally competitive leaders in innovation. Our population is more diverse, now comprising more cultures, races, religions and ethnicities than ever before. We are strengthened by this diversity.

"The principal challenges facing Indiana in our third century will include a continuing economic transformation which will require increased levels of education and innovation to be globally competitive. More money must be invested in research and development to produce new cures, products and technologies, and in continuing education reform to maximize the knowledge and skills of our people. Common-sense tax and regulatory policies also will be important, as will infrastructure enhancements. Our state will become more diverse and interconnected to the nation and the world. We must find ways to honor our rich heritage while making changes to prepare for a challenging future in the early years of our third century."

Kelli Brian

Vigo County Courthouse, Terre Haute

Indiana Voices: Edgar Whitcomb

In 2015 at the age of 97, Edgar Whitcomb was the oldest living former governor in the United States. The 43rd governor of Indiana, he served from 1969 to 1973. As an Air Force lieutenant serving in the Pacific during World War II, he was captured by the Japanese, tortured, escaped, was recaptured and escaped a second time. He swam all night through shark-infested waters to an unoccupied island, later securing passage to China, and was repatriated in December 1943. The story is told in his 1958 book, "Escape from Corregidor." After 18 years in the Indiana Senate and one term as governor, Whitcomb practiced law in Seymour, near his hometown of Hayden. He then began a series of sea adventures, sailing around the Mediterranean, across the Atlantic Ocean in 1990 and nearly sailing around the world in 1995. In 2012, he announced that he would make his retreat on 144 acres along the Ohio River near Rome available to the state of Indiana. The Gov. Edgar Whitcomb Nature Park and Retreat is one of more than 150 Bicentennial Nature Trust projects.

"Indiana is No. 1 in my life. The best place I've ever been."
~ Edgar Whitcomb

Kelly Wilkinson, The Indianapolis Star

Edgar Whitcomb looks out from the porch of his cabin in Tobinsport, along the Ohio River, in 2008.

Indiana Voices: Loretta Rush

Loretta Rush is the chief justice of the Indiana Supreme Court, sworn in on Aug. 18, 2014. She is the first woman in the state to serve in this role.

"When I look at the celebration of our bicentennial, I see 200 years of Hoosiers having access to courts in order to pursue justice. Indiana's legal roots show our state as a place where all voices are heard. In 1820, a young black woman named Polly Strong sought and won her freedom through the courts. In 1897, a lawyer named Helen Gougar argued on her own behalf before the Supreme Court that women should have a vote.

"The 1816 constitutional charge to the Court is clear, and it is my favorite part of the Indiana Constitution:

> *All courts shall be open; and every person ... shall have remedy by the due course of law.*

"The vision of accessible courts that Indiana's founding fathers articulated has not wavered. When our Constitution was significantly rewritten in 1851, the open access language was not only repeated, but expanded with the following:

> *Justice shall be administered freely, and without purchase; completely, and without denial, speedily, and without delay.*

"The voices of Strong and Gougar in Indiana courtrooms demonstrate the most basic principle envisioned by the framers of Indiana's Constitution—the courts should be a place where all Hoosiers have the opportunity to be heard and seek justice.

"What makes the courts 'open' has changed over 200 years. In 2016, we uphold the principle by providing attorneys for those with limited means, interpreters for those who don't speak English, and greater access to the courts by implementing improved technology.

"I am keenly aware, along with all of my judicial colleagues in Indiana, that we have a privilege beyond description—and the responsibility of a lifetime—to labor in the cause of justice for all Indiana citizens."

Indiana Supreme Court

Helen Gougar, who argued before the Indiana Supreme Court in 1897, and Chief Justice Loretta Rush share the same hometown—Lafayette. More than 100 years after Gougar's accomplishment, the entire Supreme Court (l to r: Robert Rucker, Brent Dickson—also of Lafayette, Loretta Rush, Mark Massa and Steven David) dedicated a historic marker in her honor. Area school children took part in the ceremony.

Ethel Brewer-McCane portrays her ancestor, Mary Bateman Clark, who was born a slave in Kentucky and successfully sued for her freedom from an indentured servitude contract in Indiana. The lawsuit, filed in 1821 in the Knox County Circuit Court in Vincennes, was eventually decided at the Indiana Supreme Court in Corydon and affirmed Indiana's legal standing on the issues of slavery and indentured servitude. Brewer-McCain dramatizes Clark's story for Indiana students through the Mary Bateman Clark Project.

Indiana Supreme Court

Five robes of the Indiana Supreme Court justices

Washington County Courthouse in Salem

Decatur County Courthouse, Greensburg, has a famous feature: a tree growing out of its tower.

A rock chiseled with "Indiana" marks the Potawatomi Trail of Death outside the Fulton County courthouse in Rochester. The Trail of Death is a Regional Historic Trail marking the forced removal of 859 members of the Potawatomi nation from Indiana to Kansas, a journey of approximately 660 miles over 61 days in which more than 40 people died and the single largest American Indian removal in Indiana history.
Shawn Pierce

Jasper County Courthouse in Rensselaer
René Stanley,
Indiana Bicentennial Commission

Indiana Voices: Abraham Lincoln

Abraham Lincoln wrote a draft autobiography in 1859, which included a short description of the family's arrival in Indiana in 1816.

"My father, at the death of his father, was but six years of age; and he grew up, literally without education. He removed from Kentucky to what is now Spencer county, Indiana, in my eighth year. We reached our new home about the time the State came into the Union. It was a wild region, with many bears and other wild animals still in the woods. There I grew up. There were some schools, so called; but no qualification was ever required of a teacher, beyond 'reading, writin, and cipherin' to the Rule of Three. If a straggler supposed to understand latin happened to sojourn in the neighborhood, he was looked upon as a wizard. There was absolutely nothing to excite ambition for education. Of course when I came of age I did not know much. Still somehow, could read, write, and cipher to the Rule of Three; but that was all."

Indiana State Library Collection

Abraham Lincoln was photographed when he returned to Indiana to campaign for Henry Clay in 1844. This is the first known photographic portrait of Lincoln.

Felicia Batman

Lincoln's Boyhood National Memorial, Lincoln City

Interior, LaGrange County Courthouse

Scott County Courthouse, Scottsburg

Hancock County Courthouse in Greenfield

Hendricks County Courthouse in Danville

Benjamin Harrison, a Republican, Indianapolis attorney and civic leader, was the 23rd president of the United States and grandson of the ninth president, William Henry Harrison.

Benjamin Harrison Presidential Site in Indianapolis

Indiana's junior senator, Dan Quayle, served as vice president of the United States 1988 to 1992.

Wendell Willkie accepts the Republican nomination for president in his hometown of Elwood on Aug. 18, 1940. Willkie lost the election to Franklin D. Roosevelt by more than 5 million votes. Willkie went on to become a pioneering advocate for civil rights and a global vision.

Randolph County Courthouse in Winchester

Rush County Courthouse in Rushville

Orange County Courthouse in Paoli

Wabash County Courthouse in Wabash

Indiana Voices: Mary Y. Snyder

Mary Y. Snyder is mayor of Cannelton, the smallest incorporated city in the state, with a population of 1,563 at the 2010 census. Located on the Ohio River, the city is home to the Cannelton Cotton Mill, a National Historic Landmark.

Perry Hammock, Indiana Bicentennial Commission

"Being a mayor is challenging. When you are mayor of a small city, it is very challenging to find revenue. We are an old town, and our infrastructure is old.

"Small towns are great because citizens will greet you on the street, wondering what the city is doing and everyone is friendly. I am the first female mayor. My first year we were able to get funds from the community and Indiana Office of Community and Rural Affairs for the start of the Cannelton River Trail, which we hope to continue. All the departments work hard to apply for all the grants possible and have received several grants from the state. One of the best came from Indiana Housing & Community Development Authority on an owner rehab program. It makes one feel good to help the citizens fix up their houses when they are in need."

Postcard of historic Cannelton

Indiana Historical Society

Tippecanoe County Courthouse in Lafayette

A civil rights leader, Richard G. Hatcher became on Jan. 1, 1968, the first African-American mayor of Gary. He was one of the first African-Americans to serve as mayor of a major U.S. city.

The Indiana National Guard is part of the larger Army National Guard and the Air National Guard. With roots dating back to 1801, the Indiana National Guard was reorganized into its current configuration in 1903. Since then the Guard has served at home and abroad as a part of multiple wars and disaster-relief actions.

Indiana Voices: Mitchell E. Daniels Jr.

©2014 Charles Jischke

Mitchell E. Daniels Jr. is Purdue University's 12th president. Daniels assumed that role in January 2013, at the conclusion of his term as governor of the state of Indiana. He was elected as the 49th governor of Indiana in 2004, in his first bid for any elected office, and was re-elected in 2008 to a second term.

"The qualities I think of as most distinctively Hoosier are a strong sense of personal responsibility, coupled with a readiness to help others when bad luck comes or when their own best efforts have proven inadequate. We expect of one another that each will pull his own weight, but in times of trouble no one is quicker to come to the aid of both friends and strangers.

"I have met firsthand Hoosiers repairing their neighbors' homes the day after a tornado; who opened their business space to a direct competitor whose facility was destroyed by a flood; who rushed unhesitatingly into the danger of a collapsed concert stage.

"On one of my 125 overnight stays in Indiana homes, I was hosted by a farmer who, while trying to remove a fallen tree trunk from railroad tracks, was struck and nearly killed. In a coma for weeks, he awoke to learn that his neighbors had planted all his fields, taken care of all his livestock, and had arranged to harvest his crops while he convalesced. 'And they wouldn't even take a dime for the fuel they used,' he told me.

"That's Indiana to me. God willing, those qualities will prove enduring through all future generations."

La Porte County Historical Society

Individuals working together create strong communities. When Mr. Glasgow of La Porte had surgery in 1955, many neighboring La Porte County farmers came to the Glasgow farm to help out.

Indiana Voices: Joe Kernan

Joe Kernan, a former mayor of South Bend, was Indiana's 47th lieutenant governor from 1997 to 2003 and the 48th governor of Indiana from 2003 to 2005.

"Our biggest challenge is and will remain our ability to fully educate and develop our citizens. It is the heart and soul of building a better Indiana.

"Education starts from the moment a child is born. Parents, guardians and communities must start by taking care of all children through nurturing and support of both physical and mental development. Every Hoosier needs to understand both how and why they must be engaged.

"Our Hoosier children have an immediate capacity to learn and these early years are critical in forming who they are as adults and what they will become. Nothing is more important for our children, their future and that of the great state of Indiana."

Students from the Indiana Math and Science Academy take a look at the original Indiana flag during Statehood Day at the Statehouse.

René Stanley,
Indiana Bicentennial Commission

By Andrew B. Takami

"It is more blessed to give than to receive" was the title of my undergraduate college commencement remarks. This biblical principle of giving was a theme woven into the fabric of my life from childhood. It was part of an educational core I was taught by my parents, and an outlook that continues to guide my life today.

Part of why I chose to pursue a career in higher education was because of my belief in the importance of philanthropy—giving more than receiving. Another reason was because of how my parents prioritized education.

The dissemination of knowledge through education, from teacher to student, is a philanthropic endeavor in the most basic sense. I have seen this dynamic through my family's history.

My father, who was raised in Honolulu, Hawaii, came to Indiana—following several years of military service in Germany—to attend a Bible school in Jeffersonville, the Christ Gospel Bible Institute.

While attending the school, he learned a new way of life. He knew education was important, so in addition to his biblical studies, he pursued the necessary certifications in the electrical vocation.

Over the years, my dad has shared how difficult it was starting out in Indiana. He knew very few people and there was little in the way of supporting communities.

Like my father, my mother also was drawn to the state because of an interest in attending the Christ Gospel Bible Institute. She moved to Indiana from DeKalb, Illinois.

Students at Trine University in Angola (formerly Tri-State University), founded in 1884, study on the lawn of the 450-acre campus.
Dean A. Orewiler for Trine University

continued

My parents met at the school in 1971. Along with their accomplishments, and with the purpose of education and spiritual growth being paramount for them, they were the first couple at the school to graduate as a husband-and-wife team.

Education continued to be something my parents embraced, which is why they chose diverse educational tracks for the K-12 education of my sister, brother and me. Now all college graduates, we gained valuable experiences through public education, private education, and even through home education.

With children of my own now, together with my wife, I recognize that educational opportunities in Indiana are greater for our children than they were in the past. My two daughters and son have the opportunity to excel and thrive on a world stage with endless possibilities.

Thanks to state support and the philanthropy of many, the future is bright for generations to come.

My mentor, J. Robert Shine of New Albany, has always stressed the importance of educational attainment and the value of investing in the future. Over the years, he has encouraged me to continue my educational advancement, while reminding me how it is my responsibility to pour best practices into others as well. I do this to the best of my ability, as I see—like him—the importance of investing in the future. This is the basic premise of a public service educational group we created some years ago known as The Windsor Society.

Throughout Indiana's 200-year history, many Hoosiers have done their part to support the educational advancement of the state without thought of receiving something in return. Today, Indiana's educators—from kindergarten teachers to college professors—understand and embody this concept.

From the very beginning, Indiana's leaders understood how access to education at all levels was an integral part of forming a solid state.

Higher education was a reality in Indiana even before the state was founded. In 1801, Territorial Gov. William Henry Harrison chartered Vincennes University as the higher-education institution for the Northwest Territory.

In 1816, Indiana's Constitution called for the development of a general educational system. The Constitution noted, "It shall be the duty of the General Assembly as soon as circumstances permit to provide by law for a general system of education, ascending in a regular graduation from township schools to a state university, wherein tuition shall be gratis and equally open to all."

"From the very beginning, Indiana's leaders understood how access to education at all levels was an integral part of forming a solid state."

It provided no firm timetable, however, and initial efforts to create a public education system were slow. By the 1840s, the illiteracy rate in Indiana was among the highest of all Northern states. Caleb Mills, the first faculty member of Wabash College in Crawfordsville, fought diligently to develop a statewide public school system.

The Indiana Constitutional Convention of 1851 passed a provision requiring the General Assembly "to provide, by law, for a general and uniform system of Common Schools, wherein tuition shall be without charge, and equally open to all." It was determined this system should be supported mostly by local tax dollars. Mills, following his success in helping to establish a public school system, went on to be named Indiana's first state school superintendent.

Like Mills, many others since then have done their part to support the dissemination of knowledge in Indiana.

Indiana University President and Chancellor Herman B Wells led Indiana University's expansion from a local university to one of national renown. Purdue University has taken a leading role in America's exploration of space. The Rev. Theodore Hesburgh, University of Notre Dame president, was at the forefront of supporting human rights throughout the world.

Andrew Carnegie, a Scottish-American industrialist who led the expansion of the steel industry in the late 19th century, was responsible for funding the construction of more Carnegie libraries in Indiana than in any other state in America. Today, these libraries—and others funded by the state—continue to bring people together and serve as institutions of knowledge. They are community centers, as Carnegie originally envisioned.

Indiana's colleges and universities have played a key role in Indiana's successes since the state's founding. The number of institutions of higher learning located in Indiana today—especially when compared with the state's population and geographic size—is truly remarkable. Many of them are consistently ranked among the top in the nation and world.

One area in which Indiana shows promise is in tailoring education to workforce needs. Today, Indiana's Regional Works Councils are meeting across the state to see how career and technical education can be better integrated as Indiana looks for renewed ways to expand educational opportunities.

Community colleges, such as Ivy Tech Community College of Indiana, are helping students from diverse backgrounds, ages and preparation levels prepare for the workforce or transition to four-year colleges and universities.

Another educational concept Indiana has supported is home schooling for K-12 students. Indiana is considered one of the most supportive states in America in this arena. Additionally, church-based schools work to celebrate and continue their religious traditions through the education of young people and in training the next generation of clergy.

As we celebrate Indiana's bicentennial and move toward the continued educational advancement of Indiana, I believe philanthropy and finding common ground are critical. There are new ways to build partnerships and alliances among Indiana's colleges and universities, K-12 educators, business and community leaders, philanthropic partners and beyond.

Indiana's bright future depends on the education we deliver today. Focusing the state's assets will be an important part of ensuring a successful future for Indiana over the next 200 years. And I believe Hoosiers embracing the biblical principle "It is more blessed to give than to receive" will continue to be paramount toward true growth and sustainability for Indiana.

Andrew B. Takami is director of Purdue Polytechnic New Albany, Purdue University.

Barbara Johnston, University of Notre Dame

University of Notre Dame president Rev. John Jenkins meets with a student on the first day of classes.

Indiana Voices: Glen Eva Dunham

Glen Eva Dunham, a teacher at Beveridge Elementary School in Gary, has taught kindergarten in her hometown school system for 28 years. She also has served her community's schools in many other ways: as president and treasurer of the Parent-Teacher Organization, as a teacher's union representative, and as a coach of the boys basketball team. She shares her thoughts about teaching kindergarten:

Walk don't run
Talk don't shout
Raise your hands
Don't call out
Put things back
When you're done
These are rules for everyone.

"This rhyme is one of the first things I teach my kindergarten students each fall. I teach them the foundations. I want them to be exposed to things they need to be exposed to, to grow academically. In the six hours we are together each day I want to teach them how to love and care for each other so they can be successful citizens in the world.

"Kindergartners are fresh, they're new—you can really mold them. They're like little sponges. When they come back after Christmas break in January you see the light bulbs go on—they start to "get it" and you can see their growth.

"We have an early-childhood program here in Gary, but not all of the children attend. Some of them start with no alphabet, their vocabulary is very limited, and by January they know almost all of their letters. They know the sounds of the alphabet and can start putting those sounds together and start making words. They can write their names and know their colors. By the end of the school year they can count to 50. My goal is to have a 'green party' at the end of the year, where all of the students reach the 'green light' milestone and get to eat green cupcakes.

"When I first started teaching, we only had half-day kindergarten, two-and-a-half hours a day. I would see 60 students a day, and all we had time for was reading, writing and arithmetic. Now we have an extended-day program and I have 30 students. I set up learning centers, small groups and extra activities so no one gets lost in the shuffle. We do motor-skills activities, learn nursery rhymes, take field trips to places like the Indiana Dunes and the zoo. We used to take a field trip once a month, but now we don't have as many of those opportunities because of the economy. I wish we had more opportunities to get out. We want to give them the opportunities that will help them be successful.

"I teach them manners, how to cross the street, how to use a computer. I try to stay current with the job and keep up with them. In the cell-phone age there are so many distractions. You try to be the mom, the social worker, the nurse. We don't have neighborhood schools anymore, so parents don't have the opportunity to come to school—their transportation and work schedules make getting here more of a challenge. But I've always lived in the neighborhood where I teach. I go to church and see the kids; I go to the grocery stores and see the kids. I see their parents at the gas station. That's special.

"I try to treat the kids like they're mine—I wouldn't do anything that I wouldn't do to my own son. I'm a disciplinarian and teach them to respect adults. But they see so much crime, the houses they have to pass by to get to school. So you try to love them, try not to be so hard on them, give them hugs. If you let them know you love them, but that you aren't going to let them get away with stuff, they're going to love you back.

"Sometimes I see former students when I'm at the mall with my son, and he says, 'Wow, these kids still remember you.' The students from my oldest class are about 35 years old now, and they come back and tell me about different incidents, tell me how I really changed them.

"I'm 59 years old, and I still get down on the rug with the kids. It's hard to get up, but I do it. I love the moments I share with them: They scream your name, you hug them, they hug you back. That's why I keep doing it."

NFact

Average Length of Indiana School Term

1866: 68 days
1879: 136 days
1900: 149 days
2015: 180 days

Indiana ranks 10th in the nation in the number of foreign students in the state.

Source: Institute of International Education, 2013

School Enrollment 2014-15

All: 1,130,285 students
Public: 1,046,026
Non-public: 84,016

Source: Indiana Department of Education

A first-grader enjoys a close encounter with a leopard gecko at Mount Comfort Elementary School in Hancock County.

Bill McCleery

Third-graders in Richmond have the opportunity to "perform" with the Richmond Symphony Orchestra.

Technology is transforming today's classrooms, and tablets are replacing textbooks in many Indiana schools. Here, kindergarten students at Park Tudor School in Indianapolis create gingerbread characters on iPads.

Fourth-graders examine artifacts at the Battle of Corydon Civil War Museum. All fourth-grade students in Indiana study the state's history as part of the curriculum.

Marian University

When students, teachers and families take field trips to the Nina Mason Pulliam EcoLab on the campus of Marian University, they participate in conservation activities such as installing native plant species.

Marcin Zalewski

Children use an electronic microscope during an educational event organized by the Sycamore Land Trust at one of its southern Indiana nature preserves.

Ralph Cooley

Local schoolchildren hear a presentation by a President Lincoln impersonator at the Jennings County Historical Society.

Indiana Voices: David Harris

David Harris is founder and CEO of The Mind Trust, an Indianapolis educational non-profit focused on creating innovative new school models.

"Indianapolis has been known for decades as an epicenter for many disciplines—from transportation to sports and auto racing to life sciences. In the 21st century, we added another accolade to the list: hub of education innovation. Our work to reshape the public K-12 system to create quality schools for all students jump-started a statewide conversation and led cities such as Nashville, Tennessee; Cincinnati, Ohio; and others to strive to replicate our achievements.

David Harris, right, with Marcus Robinson, chancellor and CEO of Tindley Accelerated Schools.

"It began in 2000, when Indianapolis Mayor Bart Peterson envisioned Indianapolis as a center for education transformation. He garnered legislative approval to become the first mayor in Indiana—and the nation—to have the authority to create charter schools: public schools that operate independently of school districts.

"Building from this work, in 2006 we created The Mind Trust, a first-of-its-kind education nonprofit whose goal is to provide all Indianapolis students the opportunity to attend a great school. Through The Mind Trust's work, new world-class schools and networks have been created in Indianapolis, and other national and local education nonprofits have been recruited to or launched in the city.

"In 2016, there are more than 30 mayor-sponsored charter schools in Indianapolis, and studies have shown that students at these charters perform better than their peers in traditional public schools. In addition, The Mind Trust has incubated and launched a host of education nonprofits and schools that are better serving Indianapolis students and schools.

"There is still much to be done, but Indianapolis is making great progress when it comes to improving public education—and Indianapolis is making a name for itself in the process."

Tindley Schools

Students at Tindley Renaissance Academy, an Indianapolis charter school for students in kindergarten through grade 4 that focuses on preparing students for college. The Charles A. Tindley Accelerated School, another in the Tindley group of schools, was one of the earliest charter schools in Indianapolis.

Now-vacant one-room schoolhouses still dot the landscapes of rural Indiana. The ghostly remnants of Green Center School occupy a Noble County field.

Children attended the College Corners School in rural DeKalb County from 1858 to 1940. Then the building sat vacant and crumbling for five decades until the Weicht family, who lived across the road, restored it.

Indiana Voices: Betsy Slavens

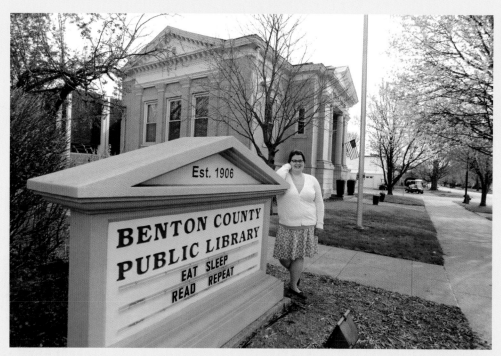

John Whalen

Betsy Slavens in front of the Benton County Public Library.

Betsy Slavens is director of the Benton County Public Library in Fowler. The library, built in 1906 at a cost of $7,500, is one of 164 Carnegie-endowed libraries—two university, 162 public—in the state.

"Indiana has more Carnegie libraries than any other state. I think this speaks volumes about the inherent generosity and frugality of Hoosiers. From 1901 to 1918, groups of citizens in 162 communities across Indiana banded together to secure the grant from the Carnegie Corporation of New York for their library buildings. In order to prove how sincere the need for the library was, the community had to agree to taxation in order to procure materials, maintain the building and provide staffing. This kind of give and take is hard to imagine in our current culture.

"Today in our world of constant technological advancement and shrinking municipal budgets, it's easy to argue that libraries aren't relevant. But for a small community, the library is the most important building in town. It's likely the only place to find a book or movie for miles. For some, it's the only place where they can reliably access the internet. Libraries provide a public place to discuss community concerns. Librarians work tirelessly to provide programming that meets community needs—early literacy preparation through preschool

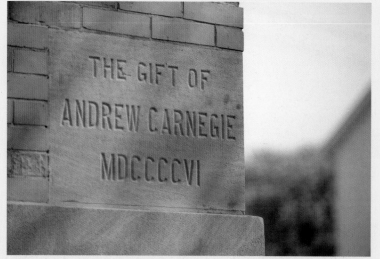

John Whalen

story hour, summer reading programs that keep children engaged throughout school breaks, and adult enrichment activities like lecture series and book and craft clubs.

"It's easy to compare a library to some dusty old relic of yesteryear. But I think a better analogy is to think of the library as your cool best friend—the one who will lend you anything without asking any questions, just as long as you promise to return it on time."

Akron Carnegie Public Library

The Akron Public Library in Fulton County celebrated its 100th anniversary in 2015. Here, residents gather for the ground-breaking of the Carnegie library on October 28, 1914.

Amanda Bortko, Amanda Claire Photography

Crown Point's first library, built in 1908 with a $12,000 grant from Andrew Carnegie. It opened with a collection of 1,500 reference and nonfiction volumes, but "very few works of the lighter sort," according to the library's history.

Shannon Malanoski

Cleo Rogers Memorial Public Library in Columbus was designed by the renowned architectural firm I.M. Pei & Partners. Pei said the project "should occupy a space which would be quiet yet dignified; that it be easily accessible to the great majority of people, both young and old; that its location create an area of urban space, and that it take into consideration the future growth of the community and its character."

John Whalen

The Manuscript Room of the Indiana State Library, which was designed by Indianapolis architectural firm Pierre & Wright.

Indiana Voices: Dr. Richard L. Ludwick

Dr. Richard L. Ludwick is president and CEO of Independent Colleges of Indiana, which represents independent colleges throughout the state. He grew up in Randolph County, on a farm near Union City.

Independent Colleges of Indiana

Dr. Richard Ludwick meets with a college senior.

"I have been a history buff, and in particular Indiana history, my whole life. I remember as a kid poring over accounts of the Indian wars and painstakingly reenacting key battles with toy figures. I later went on to major in history at one of our ICI member colleges. As president of the Independent Colleges of Indiana, I've often thought about the connections between the histories of our private, nonprofit colleges and universities and the history of our state.

"Each of Indiana's 31 independent colleges and universities has its own special story, traditions and student-centered focus. However, what their unique stories have in common with one another—and with the story of Indiana's own 200 years of statehood—is that they are all built on the foundation of liberty (independence) and enlightenment (education).

"On the Indiana state flag, this spirit of independent enlightenment is exemplified by the burning torch, radiating light out onto surrounding stars. For our independent colleges and universities, it is exemplified through the lives and contributions of the millions of their graduates who have shaped, are now shaping, and will continue to shape their own individual stories and Indiana's larger story. They are guardians, torchbearers, of that Hoosier ideal of liberty and enlightenment—individuals free to discover, learn and innovate, lighting the way to our shared future."

The James S. Markiewicz Solar Energy Research Facility at Valparaiso University offers undergraduate students and faculty an opportunity to conduct research with one of only five solar furnaces in the United States. In 2013, the research team secured a $2.3 million cooperative agreement from the U.S. Department of Energy to fund solar research.

Jon L. Hendricks, Valparaiso University

A performance during alumni weekend at Bethel College, a Mennonite school that opened in Mishawaka in 1947.

Peter Ringenberg, Bethel College

Students take to the books in the Emmaus dining room at Ancilla College, a two-year private liberal arts college established in 1937. The school's 1,200-acre campus in the town of Donaldson is shared by Ancilla College and the American Headquarters of the Poor Handmaids of Jesus Christ.

Mark Shephard, Shephard Imageworks

Springtime brings the possibility of outdoor classes at DePauw University in Greencastle. The four-year liberal arts college was founded by the Methodist Church as Asbury College in 1837. East College, shown in this photo, was dedicated in 1877 and remains in use today.

Larry Ligget, DePauw University

153

It's a family affair during Taylor University commencement ceremonies in Upland.

James R. Garringer

A student watches a demonstration of the ancient art of calligraphy on the campus of Hanover College. Indiana's first private college, it was founded in 1827 near the banks of the Ohio River.

Hanover College

The Shell Chapel at St. Mary-of-the-Woods College near Terre Haute, the nation's oldest Catholic liberal arts college for women. St. Mother Theodore Guerin established an academy for girls that in 1846 was granted the first charter for the higher education of women in the state. The college introduced one of the first independent study programs in the nation, the Women's External Degree Program, in 1973. In 2015, the school announced it would become fully coeducational.

Christina Blust

Students conduct an experiment at Wabash College in Crawfordsville. Founded in 1832, the college is one of only three remaining all-male liberal arts colleges in the nation.

Dancers perform in silhouette at Butler University dance department's annual midwinter ballet in Clowes Memorial Hall.

Indiana University's limestone Sample Gates are an iconic site in Bloomington.

Ivy Tech Community College of Indiana, founded in 1963, is the state's largest public postsecondary institution and the nation's largest singly accredited statewide community college system. It serves nearly 200,000 students annually at 32 degree-granting locations throughout Indiana, including its Northeast campus in Fort Wayne, pictured here. Ivy Tech also offers classes in more than 75 communities.

Jaclyn Y. Garver

Indiana Voices: John Norberg

Purdue University is known worldwide for its aviation and aeronautics programs. Recently, Purdue University President Mitch Daniels announced plans to create a 980-acre Purdue Research Park Aerospace District in West Lafayette. Purdue Archivist John Norberg offers a glimpse into Purdue's role in aviation and aeronautic history.

NASA

Astronaut, Crown Point native and Purdue graduate Jerry Ross

"Sixty-one years before Purdue University graduate Neil Armstrong stepped on the moon, another Boilermaker put his own mark on the history of flight.

"Cliff Turpin of Dayton, Ohio, graduated from Purdue in 1908 with a degree in mechanical engineering and built motorcycles with his father before joining Orville and Wilbur Wright to develop and demonstrate flight to a skeptical nation. Turpin's work launched more than a century of Purdue involvement in flight.

"In addition to educating countless engineers who played key roles in the rapid advancement of aerospace, Purdue produced pilots who became legends: Frederick Martin, who—while he did not finish—planned, organized and led the first round-the-world flight in 1924; George Welch, who studied at Purdue and in 1948 officially became the second person in the world to break the sound barrier; and Iven Kincheloe, who in 1956 was the first person called "spaceman" when he flew the Bell X-2 at record speeds and heights.

"Amelia Earhart, the first woman and the second person to fly the Atlantic Ocean solo, worked at Purdue as an adviser to engineering and a counselor on careers for women students from 1935 to 1936. The Purdue Research Foundation helped to finance her final flight and the Barron Hilton Flight and Space Archives at Purdue contains the world's largest collection of Earhart material.

"NASA has selected 23 Purdue graduates as astronauts, including Armstrong and Gene Cernan, the first and last people on the moon. Virgil "Gus" Grissom traveled from Mitchell, Indiana to Purdue and went on to become the second American in space. He died in January 1967 along with Purdue graduate Roger Chaffee during a test of the first Apollo capsule.

A Purdue University graduate in electrical engineering who received his doctor of medicine degree from Indiana University, Indianapolis native David Wolf has spent 168 days in space, including 128 days on the Mir Space Station.

"Nineteen Purdue astronauts flew on space shuttles, including Jerry Ross of Crown Point, who—along with one other person—holds the world record of seven space launches."

Students at Purdue University's Zucrow Laboratories perform propulsion-related research on rockets and gas-turbine engines.

Purdue University, Mark Simons

Paean For A New Library

...It came to pass that
man and wo/man
rose from their crouching
Stood upon their legs and
     walked
In time, styli and brush in hand
They scribed on scroll and on papyri
    a legacy of circumstance
  of deeds, of dreams, and dance

And soon the wise ones said we
    need a shelter
where children can come
to bathe in Light
surrounded by wisdom their
    minds challenged
their spirits renewed....
Whereon, the women and the men
created such a haven

And the darkness glowed
For in it they stored sunlight
and water, pastures and plains
snowcrowned mountains raging
storms and circling galaxies
And the people of Alexandria, of Carthage
Then of Rome, of Paris, of New York,
and the Heartland of America each
in their own time, stood around it
    and marvelled
For through the luminescence shone the
records of their living, their loving
their anguish, joy, their poetry
their song

We reverence libraries for they hold the past
Contain the blueprints for our future
the impetus toward present possibility....
A beleaguered society, when that society is chaotic
must rush first to defend its children and then
    to secure its libraries

There comes a time when a need is met
a haven prepared, a library built
When the people gather, to reverence and
    re-visit
For libraries are fortress
    and wooded stream
    challenge and surcease....
Repositories of revolution, and of respite
  Staunch
    Enduring
     In them
we find the people's substance, their spirit
  their brilliances and delusions
    their visions
    and their Truths

    In the end
it is the people, empowered, who prevail
who are their own Enlightenment who
    secure inclusion
Who are their own beneficent result

    ~ Mari Evans

On the occasion of the dedication of the Indianapolis downtown
library building
© Mari Evans 2007

*The atrium of the Indianapolis Central
Library, dedicated in 2007. The original
building was completed in 1917.*
John Whalen

By David Lawther Johnson

For Hoosiers, success on the field—and in many fields—has always been a team sport. Whether on high school basketball courts, high-production farms for corn and soybeans, or busy factory floors turning out state-of-the art aircraft engines, Hoosiers excel when we work in teams.

Certainly, it takes terrific teamwork to advance the health care economy that powers Indiana today. Work we do in teams—making medicines, developing implantable devices like vascular stents and artificial hips, producing better seeds and crops, and deploying sophisticated diagnostic technologies—all adds up to $60 billion in economic impact every year, and rising fast.

Indiana exports cars and trucks and aircraft engines around the world; but other than California, we ship more health care-related products than any other state. Taken together, medicine and health—life sciences and health care—account for nearly 850,000 employees and $15 billion in annual wages at the turn of Indiana's third century. It's no small wonder that this productive sector puts Indiana in the very top tier of all 50 states when it comes to the important work of discovering novel therapies, manufacturing new medical products and delivering better health care to patients here at home—and around the world.

From its beginnings 140 years ago, something even more basic than teamwork has sparked this huge piece of Indiana's economic engine. Great innovators and entrepreneurs have provided Indiana's real competitive advantage. In 1876, Col. Eli Lilly, a Civil War veteran and pharmacist, set up shop as a chemist. Creativity consistently typified Lilly's products—gelatin capsules and fruit flavors for liquid medicines are two of many innovations attributed

The third annual Monumental Yoga event on Monument Circle in Indianapolis drew more than 1,000 people.
Amanda Reynolds

continued

to this founder of what is today one of the largest pharmaceutical enterprises in the world. And innovation has continued to distinguish the Lilly brand, whether with the first successful development of human insulin in the 1920s, the first mass production of polio vaccines in the 1950s, the discovery of whole new generations of antibiotics in the 1970s, the commercialization of the first biotechnology products to treat diabetes in the 1980s, the delivery of groundbreaking therapies for depression and mental illness in the 1990s, or breakthrough discoveries in the treatment of complex cancers and neurological disorders like Alzheimer's disease in the 2000s.

Meanwhile and to the north, the remarkable story of tiny Warsaw, Indiana, as home to a full third of the world's $40 billion orthopedics industry, also began with a single resourceful entrepreneur. In the late 19th century, Revra DePuy was a traveling salesman and trained chemist who experimented with many things, including new tech-

Indiana exports cars and trucks and aircraft engines around the world; but other than California, we ship more health care-related products than any other state.

niques for sugar-coating pills and improving splints for broken bones. The splint market proved especially inviting, since the preferred treatment materials at the time were wooden staves ripped from barrels, arriving in limited shapes with abundant splinters. DePuy developed a special fiber splint for the purpose and quickly found a flourishing market among the many visitors to Warsaw and nearby Winona Lake, site of the "religious Chautauquas" of the Reverend Billy Sunday and other evangelical preachers of the day. He opened DePuy Manufacturing in Warsaw in 1895, and the company quickly flourished. DePuy's sales leader, Justin Zimmer, contributed mightily to that growth, but he also grew frustrated with his opportunities for advancement. After his wife suggested he would forever be "just small potatoes" unless he set out on his own, Zimmer did just that and began Zimmer Manufacturing in 1926. Fifty years later, a similar spirit drove Zimmer employee Dane Miller and three partners to establish another new orthopedics manufacturer, Biomet. The three companies founded by these entrepreneurs ended up putting Warsaw onto the map as the "Orthopedics Capital of the World," today employing nearly 7,000 workers in a town of scarcely 14,000 inhabitants.

And in the world of medical engineering and devices, Indiana proved fertile ground well beyond orthopedic implants. In the early 1960s, a young hospital products entrepreneur from Canton, Illinois, found himself in Bloomington, Indiana. Bill Cook liked it here, and decided to stay. In 1963, he and his wife, Gayle, started a catheter company in the spare bedroom of their Bloomington apartment, investing in plastic tubing and a blowtorch to solder iron for their first products. The company began to grow, especially after Cook teamed up with one of the early pioneers of minimally invasive surgery, and developed hundreds of new products for repairing blood vessels, opening clogged arteries with stents, repairing wounds and even growing new tissue. Eventually, the Cook Group became the world's largest privately held medical device company, employing nearly 5,000 Hoosiers.

As the Cooks were busy building a medical engineering capital in Bloomington, another restless young engineer in Indianapolis named Willard "Bill" Eason was deciding to leave the comforts of a steady job at Ford Motor Company to start a new business. Founded in Eason's garage in 1964, Bio-Dynamics Inc. sought to develop new kinds of diagnostic products to assist physicians in accurately analyzing and addressing the health of their patients. Through development and a series of acquisitions, Eason's company grew over the next three decades to become the North American headquarters for Roche Diagnostics, employing 3,000 Hoosiers as the largest diagnostics company in the United States and a world leader in diabetes monitoring and personalized medicine.

The vision of these six Hoosiers (by birth or by choice) has made Indiana today not only one of the largest but also one of the most diversified centers of life sciences economic activity anywhere in the world. Add in the plant-science prowess of Dow AgroSciences (itself, in part, a spinoff from Col. Lilly's company); the IU School of Medicine, the nation's largest medical school and home to frontier research, such as Dr. Larry Einhorn's groundbreaking discoveries for treating cancer; and one of America's leading health care delivery markets—and it's clear why Indiana's future, as well as its past, will be all about finding and delivering new ways for people to live better, longer and healthier lives.

And while Indiana's health care history features an impressive array of rugged individuals, the companies they founded fully embrace the traditional Hoosier values of collaboration and teamwork—and generosity. In no other state have leading health care and life sciences companies, working closely with distinguished research universities and major philanthropic foundations, come together to form a collaborative enterprise like BioCrossroads, established in 2004. So far, BioCrossroads has raised more than $300 million to develop talent, build enterprises and fund new companies to accelerate Indiana's health care growth. New exciting collaborations, especially the Indiana Biosciences Research Institute, are on the horizon.

Equally rare, the founders as well as the employees of the companies they created have given back to their communities from the very beginning. The historic preservation of West Baden Hotel and Old Centrum Church by Bill and Gayle Cook; the restoration of Winona Lake by Dane and Mary Louise Miller; and the establishment of the Lilly Endowment by Col. Lilly's descendants Eli Lilly, J.K. Lilly Sr. and J.K. Lilly Jr. as one of the largest charitable foundations in the world, focused intently on Indiana's prosperity—these are also among the lasting contributions to us all by the drivers of this industry.

A growing economy built upon innovation in health care: It's a legacy—and a promise—to make all Hoosiers proud.

David Johnson is president and CEO of BioCrossroads, which encourages collaboration and strategic investments to enhance Indiana's life sciences economy

Kevin Foster

NFact

Investments from all sources in Indiana health sciences firms topped $100 million in 2014, a giant leap from just over $30 million the previous year.

Source: BioEnterprise 2014 Midwest Healthcare Growth Capital Report

Marian University

Marian University's College of Osteopathic Medicine, which accepted its first class in 2013, is housed in the Michael A. Evans Center for Health Sciences. Evans, CEO of Indianapolis-based AIT Laboratories, donated $48 million to the school, which was founded to help alleviate a physician shortage in Indiana.

Indiana Voices: Kyle Bonham

Kyle Bonham, program manager at IU Health LifeCare, provides HIV care and prevention services to more than 1,300 HIV-positive patients as well as those at risk for contracting the virus. Two high-school trips to Africa spurred his interest in social work.

"I saw IU Health LifeCare as my opportunity to continue working with HIV, although this would be my first domestic experience with it.

"It allowed me to work in the medical field (and work very closely with medical providers), work with a misunderstood and often stigmatized patient population, and give back to the community in which I live on a daily basis.

"Those who are underserved tend to be misunderstood. Poverty, substance abuse, homelessness and mental illness often go hand in hand. These are populations that society often overlooks.

"Working in the social service field has its ups and downs—the highs tend to be really high, and the lows tend to be really low. I wouldn't change it for anything, though."

Indiana University Richard M. Fairbanks School of Public Health

Members of the faculty of the Indiana University Richard M. Fairbanks School of Public Health gathered in 2014 as part of the first official World Heart Day observance in the United States. Raising awareness about heart disease is just one goal of the school, which opened in 2012 to tackle critical public health problems affecting Hoosiers.

Purdue University Professor Kinam Park, president of Akina Inc., one of the companies in the Purdue Research Park, holds vials containing polymers that are used for drug delivery systems and biomedical engineering. Akina has synthesized and commercialized hundreds of polymers that are distributed worldwide for developing products ranging from nanoparticles to 3D cell printing.
Vincent Walter

Indianapolis physician Jean Miller laughs with some young patients at one of Timmy Global Health's medical clinics in the Amazon Basin in Ecuador. Timmy Global Health exports Hoosier compassion, sending approximately 40 medical service teams abroad each year to provide consistent, quality health care services to rural and underserved communities.
Gabrielle Cheikh Photography

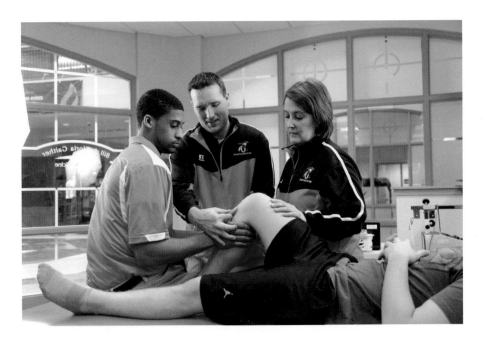

The Anderson University Department of Kinesiology offers preparation for careers in athletic training, exercise science, coaching and teaching physical education.
Anderson University

Indiana Voices: Kim Irwin

Kim Irwin is executive director of Health by Design, which works to ensure that communities throughout Indiana have neighborhoods, public spaces and transportation infrastructure that promote physical activity and healthy living.

Kim Irwin

Kim Irwin with an Indiana Pacers Bikeshare bike, one of many initiatives in Indianapolis to facilitate physical activity.

"Recent studies show that if you line up 10 Hoosiers, six of them would be overweight—three to the point of obesity.

"While many people see such statistics and think of fried food and soft drinks, I think of neighborhoods without sidewalks. Neighborhoods with community destinations—jobs, schools, medical services, shopping and parks—that can be reached only by car.

"Over the past several decades, we've built our communities with little regard for people traveling by foot, bike or transit. Now we have neighborhoods without sidewalks, retail services on the edge of town, and schools far away from where students actually live.

"The result? Hoosiers suffer from the side effects of sedentary living: obesity, related chronic illnesses and poor mental health. We know that, just as certainly as our car-centric ways have negatively affected our health, communities that promote active living can improve it.

"When Hoosiers have access to sidewalks, trails and bikeways, they use them, incorporating physical activity into their day-to-day routine. Build it and they will come… on foot and in better health."

The Susan G. Komen Race for the Cure raises money annually in several Indiana cities for breast cancer research.

Shannon Malanoski

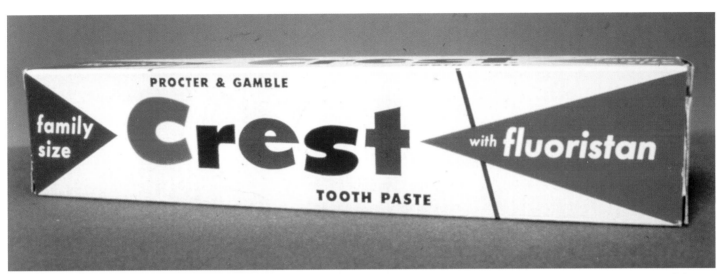

Indiana University researchers discovered how to fluoridate toothpaste, resulting in today's ubiquitous Crest brand.

Eli Lilly and Co. researchers regularly collaborate with private and public partners to bring new therapies to market.

Gerald Abel, Bass Photo

▌NFact

The Breathalyzer was invented in 1953 by Indiana University forensic scientist Robert Borkenstein.

Eli Lilly and Co. in 1923 became the first company to mass-produce insulin for the treatment of diabetes.

Eli Lilly and Co.

Indiana Voices: Teresa Hutton

Teresa Hutton is obstetrics nurse manager at Greene County General Hospital, which is observing Indiana's bicentennial with a program to fight infant mortality.

Greene County General Hospital

Greene County General Hospital's Obstetrics Nurse Manager Teresa Hutton and Chief Nursing Officer Lea Ann Camp.

"Babies born in Indiana's bicentennial year, 2016, should have the best chance to survive and thrive as lifelong Hoosiers. With the state's unacceptably high infant mortality rate, it is more difficult than ever to promise that to our smallest citizens. Greene County General Hospital's Sweet Dreams Baby Bundles can help change that. We want our bicentennial babies to be the strongest and healthiest babies ever, and we hope to combat the rate of infant mortality by encouraging expectant mothers to complete a continuum of prenatal care with Greene County General Hospital. After completing our program and delivering their babies in our state-of-the art obstetrics wing, new mothers will go home not only with their bundle of joy but with a fully equipped 'baby bundle' as well.

"The 'bundles' consist of a large, heavy-duty cardboard box, whimsically and tastefully decorated, lined with a waterproof mattress, a cover and a sheet, all designed to promote safe sleep for new infants. Other items included in the box are onesies, diapers, blankets and educational material covering tobacco cessation and safe-sleep practices. This program is based on the famous Finnish baby boxes, which have played a huge part in reducing that country's infant mortality rate from 65 deaths per 1,000 live births when they were introduced in 1938 to just three deaths per 1,000 live births today.

"Thanks to initial funding from our local REMC (UDWI), and the generous contribution of the Greene County Foundation's Women of Worth program, we hope to make 2016 the year of healthy babies at Greene County General Hospital, celebrating our proud heritage and bright future."

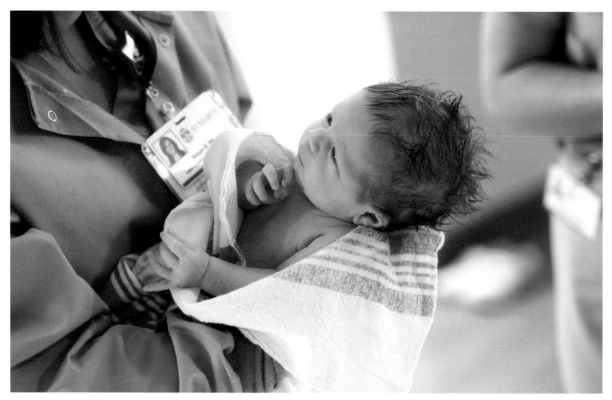

Todd Joyce

St. Mary's Hospital for Women & Children in Evansville is one of many health facilities across the state offering the prenatal care that results in healthy babies.

William Dellenback,
The Kinsey Institute for Research in Sex, Gender, and Reproduction

Human sexuality research conducted at Indiana University by Professor Alfred Kinsey gained national attention in the 1940s and 1950s. Though his work was controversial, some credit Kinsey with exploding sexual myths and bringing the discussion of sexuality into the scientific realm.

Indianapolis Business Journal

Indiana University School of Medicine faculty member Dr. Lawrence Einhorn in 1974 discovered a treatment regimen for testicular cancer that turned a 95-percent mortality rate for the disease into a 95-percent survival rate. Today, Einhorn and his colleagues are studying survivors to find ways to reduce the toxic side-effects of treatment.

NFact

The St. Vincent Heart Center was named one of the top 50 heart hospitals in the country five times by Truven Health Analytics based on claims data from the country's major health insurers.

Indianapolis Business Journal

Anthem Inc., based in Indianapolis, is the second-largest health insurance company in the country based on premiums collected.

NFact

Riley Hospital for Children at IU Health is ranked by U.S. News & World Report as the 22nd best hospital in the country for pediatric cardiology.

167

The new Sidney and Lois Eskenazi Hospital in Indianapolis was made possible, in part, by a $40 million gift from the Eskenazis, a local family. The gift was one of the largest ever made to a public hospital in the United States.

Smoking and second-hand smoke have been recognized as threats to public health in Indiana, where smoking is prohibited in most indoor public spaces.

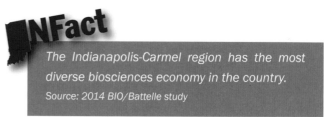

INFact

The Indianapolis-Carmel region has the most diverse biosciences economy in the country.
Source: 2014 BIO/Battelle study

The Eskenazi Health Sky Farm is the result of a partnership with Growing Places Indy, a not-for-profit that encourages urban agriculture and healthy eating. The produce raised on the hospital roof is available to patients, staff and visitors.

Dr. Peter Armstrong, chief medical officer of Warsaw-based OrthoPediatrics Corp., oversees the development of orthopedic products exclusively designed for young patients. With distribution in 30 countries, it's one of the companies responsible for Warsaw being known as the orthopedics capital of the world.

The interesting architecture of the Cook Biotech building in West Lafayette hints at the cutting edge medical research that takes place inside. Cook Biotech products have been used in more than 1.5 million soft-tissue-repair treatments worldwide.

By Gene Tempel

When I was a child in 1954, my house near St. Meinrad burned. The local volunteer fire department, organized through St. Meinrad Archabbey, tried to contain the fire. Volunteers from the community, mostly organized through the St. Meinrad Parish, provided food, clothing and other amenities. Religion and philanthropy came together.

My experience 62 years ago is repeated in communities large and small across Indiana as we celebrate Indiana's bicentennial. The volunteer fire department is alive and well in many communities. Local churches provide social services, operate schools, sponsor food banks, sponsor immigrants. Formal and organized informal philanthropy are part of every community. Many nonprofit organizations in Indiana have no staff and are not incorporated, offering no tax benefits for charitable contributions.

On the other hand, Indiana is home to Lilly Endowment Inc., one of the nation's largest private foundations. Its grant-making activities support religion, education and community development, with a special emphasis on Indiana. Its impact is all around us, from Indianapolis to every county in Indiana where Lilly Endowment has fostered the development of local community foundations to stimulate philanthropy alongside local efforts in volunteerism and philanthropy.

Indiana has a rich tradition in philanthropy. It begins with the native peoples who inhabited Indiana. Their sense of community and concern for future generations are core concepts of philanthropy. The early religious impact on philanthropy can be found in the religious schools and colleges across the state, from Notre Dame to Butler

continued

The interior of the Basilica of the Sacred Heart, Notre Dame
Heather Ziliak

to Hanover. Indiana boasts 31 private colleges and universities, almost all with an origin in the philanthropic commitment to education (and religious purposes as well). Philanthropy to support public and private education has become so important that the state provides a tax credit to individuals and corporations to encourage gifts to colleges and universities, including seminaries. Churches and religious orders traditionally supported education, health care, and the care of widows and orphans. That tradition is clearly reflected in Indiana. In addition to the private colleges in Indiana, one can still find private hospitals across the state even if they today are affiliated with larger health networks.

The variety of religious organizations in our state speaks to the diversity and importance of religion to the people of Indiana and to their philanthropic traditions. Three Benedictine monasteries, the St. Meinrad Archabbey, the Sisters of St. Benedict at Ferdinand and Our Lady of Grace Monastery in Beech Grove, practice the Benedictine value of hospitality and taking in strangers, one of the earliest forms of philanthropy.

Catholic priests are educated at St. Meinrad Seminary. The Lutheran Church-Missouri Synod has one of its two seminaries in Fort Wayne. The Christian Theological Seminary in Indianapolis is related to the Disciples of Christ. Grace Brethren Church supports a seminary at Grace Theological Seminary. And there is a Quaker seminary at Earlham College.

Indiana is also home to a range of religious headquarters. The Islamic Society of North America is headquartered in Plainfield. The Christian Church (Disciples of Christ), the Free Methodist Church, and the Wesleyan Church have their headquarters in Indianapolis. Anderson is home to the headquarters of the Church of God. Winona Lake is home to the Fellowship of Grace Brethren Churches. Huntington is home of the Church of the United Brethren in Christ. And the Friends United Meeting of the Religious Society of Friends, the largest branch of the American Quakers, is based in Richmond.

Hoosiers are noted for hospitality and helping each other. Barn raisings and grain threshing were community events. When disaster strikes today, local chapters of the Red Cross and the United Way, local community foundations, churches and Hoosiers come together to help make things better, just as the St. Meinrad community did in my case 62 years ago.

Notable civic leaders and philanthropists help set the tone for philanthropy. Eli Lilly not only was a great corporate and civic leader, he was a volunteer and philanthropist. His leadership and example as a volunteer were exemplified during the 1913 flood in Indianapolis. William and Gayle Cook not only built one of Indiana's most significant businesses in Cook Group Inc., they also devoted their time, talent and philanthropy to preserving historic places across the state, most notably the West Baden Springs and French Lick Springs Hotels. And Madam C.J. Walker developed a significant business in African-American hair care, became the first African-American woman millionaire in the U.S. and then become a noted philanthropist herself. Every community can point to leaders in volunteering time, talent and resources to engage members of the community in helping each other.

The Indiana University Lilly Family School of Philanthropy, located at Indiana University-Purdue University Indianapolis (IUPUI), conducts research on philanthropy and nonprofit organizations, conducts academic programs and provides training. The school houses the Lake Institute on Faith & Giving, dedicated to better understanding of the connection between religion and philanthropy.

"The variety of religious organizations in our state speaks to the diversity and importance of religion to the people of Indiana and to their philanthropic traditions."

Every public and private college and university campus in the state has a service-learning program supported by Indiana Campus Compact to help students understand the role of volunteering to create a better community. They sponsor alternative spring breaks to engage students in service projects. Elementary and high schools across the state engage students in service. And churches continue to teach service and philanthropy through youth mission and service projects.

The next generation of Hoosiers likely will do things differently, but they will be engaged philanthropically. They like giving and volunteering with others. They want to engage directly with recipients: tutoring students, for example. They may give online (remember the Ice Bucket Challenge?). There may be more fundraising activities like Brackets for Good, an Indiana-based charitable organization that hosts single-elimination competitive fundraising tournaments, founded by Butler University alumni Matt McIntyre and Matt Duncan and their friend, Dave Cornelius.

Research done by the Lilly Family School of Philanthropy shows that philanthropy for the environment and animals continue to grow rapidly, as does interest in international aid. Women's Philanthropy Institute research shows that women give differently than men. And research also indicates that some ethnic groups prefer to give and volunteer informally instead of through formal organizations. Immigrants impact the face of philanthropy as well, bringing with them philanthropic traditions from their own countries. Diversity in giving will reflect diversity in the population.

Philanthropy is stimulated by a vision for the future that improves on the present. Its primary roles are to reduce human suffering and enhance human potential. Often, these two roles overlap. Homeless shelters primarily reduce human suffering; museums and arts organizations primarily enhance human potential. Universities educate the next generation, thus enhancing human potential, but also conduct research that reduces human suffering.

When Indiana celebrates its next major birthday, it will have much to celebrate in religion and philanthropy as well. According to the Lake Institute, it's likely the ways in which these two powerful aspects of our lives come together in communities across Indiana will be more diverse than they are today and will have different emphases.

But some traditions will continue. Like many small Indiana towns, St. Meinrad is an unincorporated community. Its volunteer fire department likely will still be housed at St. Meinrad Archabbey. And citizens will still keep the town clean by organizing volunteer trash pickup at 8:30 every Saturday morning.

Gene Tempel is founding dean of the Lilly Family School of Philanthropy at Indiana University, the world's first school dedicated to the study and teaching of philanthropy. He led the Indiana University Foundation as its seventh president from 2008 until 2012, after 25 years of nonprofit leadership, administration and fundraising experience.

Krista Hall, St. Meinrad Archabbey

Dogwood trees bloom outside Monte Cassino Shrine at St. Meinrad Archabbey.

Indiana Voices: Felipe Martinez

Felipe Martinez is a Presbyterian minister who lives in Indianapolis and supported the start of two small bilingual Presbyterian Church USA congregations in Indianapolis and Fort Wayne.

"There have been immigrant churches in Indiana dating back to the state's early history, but the phenomenon of Latin American immigrant congregations since the beginning of the 21st century offers new insights into the religious life of this unique Hoosier community.

"The significant growth of the Latino community in Indiana has been documented in the 2000 and 2010 U.S. Census. Latinos, whether recent immigrants or U.S. born, identify themselves mostly as Roman Catholic (attending usually large parishes), though there is a growing Protestant affiliation (attending usually small congregations).

Felipe Martinez

Rev. Fernando Rodriguez, organizing pastor for Nueva Creacion, a bilingual congregation of the Presbytery of Whitewater, offers the sacrament of Communion to Victor Silva.

"As with earlier immigrant groups, Latino church members promote strong family ties and gravitate toward churches where other Latinos attend, likely because of their cultural and linguistic context. Latino congregations play a vital role in connecting recent immigrants to the culture at large because the church remains a highly trusted institution. Ministry by Latino congregations in Indiana tends to be bilingual (either offering Spanish worship for recent immigrants with English Christian education for children or grandchildren of that first generation, or offering bilingual worship services). Historically other immigrant churches saw their language-specific worship disappear quickly in favor of English as the primary language, but bilingual ministry is likely to remain a part of Latino congregations in the near future. This is due in part to an increasing acceptance of multiculturalism in society, to the continuing flow of Latino immigrants to Indiana (from abroad and within the U.S.) and to the unprecedented ability of these immigrants to remain connected to their family and culture via telephone, the Internet and the media."

IN Fact

Religious Composition of Indiana

72 percent	Christian
1 percent	Jewish
<1 percent	Muslim
<1 percent	Buddhist
<1 percent	Hindu
26 percent	Unaffiliated

Among Indiana Christians

31 percent Evangelical Protestant

16 percent Mainline Protestant

5 percent Historically Black Protestant

18 percent Catholic

1 percent Mormon

<1 percent Orthodox Christian

<1 percent Jehovah's Witness

<1 percent other Christian

Source: Pew Research Center, 2015

Hong Yin

Church of Jesus Christ of Latter Day Saints Temple under construction in Carmel.

Sue Siefert, Sisters of St. Francis

Oldenburg Franciscan Motherhouse, Oldenburg. The congregation of the Sisters of St. Francis was founded in a log cabin in 1851 by 24-year-old Sister Theresa Hacklemeier, who traveled alone from her convent in Vienna, Austria to help teach the German-speaking children and care for orphans who lost parents in the 1847 cholera epidemic.

John Kofodimos

Sunday of the Cross, celebrated at Holy Apostles Greek Orthodox Church, Carmel

Indiana Voices: Rev. Ron Johnson

Rev. Ron Johnson Jr. is senior pastor of Living Stones Church in Crown Point and director of the Indiana Pastors Alliance, a network of churches, clergy and Christian organizations that seeks to "bring biblical solutions to contemporary social problems."

"Religious freedom is the lifeblood of self-government, an essential condition for a free and democratic society, and the cornerstone of our American form of government. It was deemed so precious and essential to public life that it was enshrined in our Constitution and given the place of preeminence as the first freedom in our Bill of Rights.

"Both our republic and our state have survived and thrived for more than two centuries because men and women of courage, conviction and deep commitment to the cause of freedom were willing, like our forefathers, to make whatever sacrifices were necessary so that their children would know the blessings of liberty.

"Life, liberty and marriage and family are central issues of importance to the health of our nation. For me, these topics are incredibly serious. I call it the holy trinity of engagement: faith, family and religious freedom are the cornerstone of building a healthy society. Hoosiers are family folks, who recognize the importance of marriage and family. They also recognize that religious liberty isn't just for Christian people, it is for all people. That's what makes Indiana a great state."

James A. Strain

Badger Grove Community Baptist Church in White County

St. Paul's Episcopal Church, Indianapolis

Shabbat at Congregation Beth-El Zedeck's Early Childhood Center in Indianapolis

Stained glass window in the interior of Trinity Lutheran Church, Lebanon

Sculpted figures created by artisans from India adorn one of the towers atop the new Hindu Temple of Central Indiana. For nearly 10 years, much of Indianapolis' growing Hindu population worshipped in a temporary space until a $10 million temple expansion, which includes a worship hall with 17 shrines. On holidays, the temple draws more than 1,000 devotees.

Indiana Voices: Phil Dabagia

Phil Dabagia is president of the board of directors of The Islamic Center of Michigan City, founded in 1911 and one of the oldest mosques in the United States. His father came to Michigan City around 1910 from what was then called Syria, in modern-day Lebanon, with four brothers. After five years or so, three of the brothers returned to their homeland, while Dabagia's father and uncle remained. Dabagia grew up in Michigan City and, after serving in the Army, returned to work as a police officer and detective, retiring as assistant director of Community Corrections for La Porte County. He and his wife have three adult children and three grandchildren.

"Our mosque was founded to be a center for religion and culture. We have Friday prayers, lectures and celebrate the holidays together with about 100 families, so it is pretty sizeable. Faith, family and marriage have been very important in our community. We are very fortunate: Many of our families have been here since the turn of the century and people know us and accept us as part of the community. In Michigan City, there were immigrants of every kind: Irish, German, Italian. Muslims here got along great with the local Maronite Catholics, who also came from Syria and Lebanon.

"Islam is a religion of peace. A true Muslim is peaceful. There are 1.3 billion Muslims in the world, and it is not a new religion. It hasn't changed, and you don't change it. We pray five times each day, the way scripture instructs us. If people had a better understanding of other faiths, we would have fewer problems. It's the idea of learning to get along that is important."

The Islamic Center of Michigan City

Megan Hopper

Candlelight worshippers at St. Mary Queen of Peace, Danville

Dianne Conrad Stoner Gustin

Country church in Miami County at Christmas

Daniel R. Patmore

Usher Festus Obanor checks over his bulletins during a brief pause in parishioners entering the sanctuary for Sunday services at Nazarene Baptist Church in Evansville.

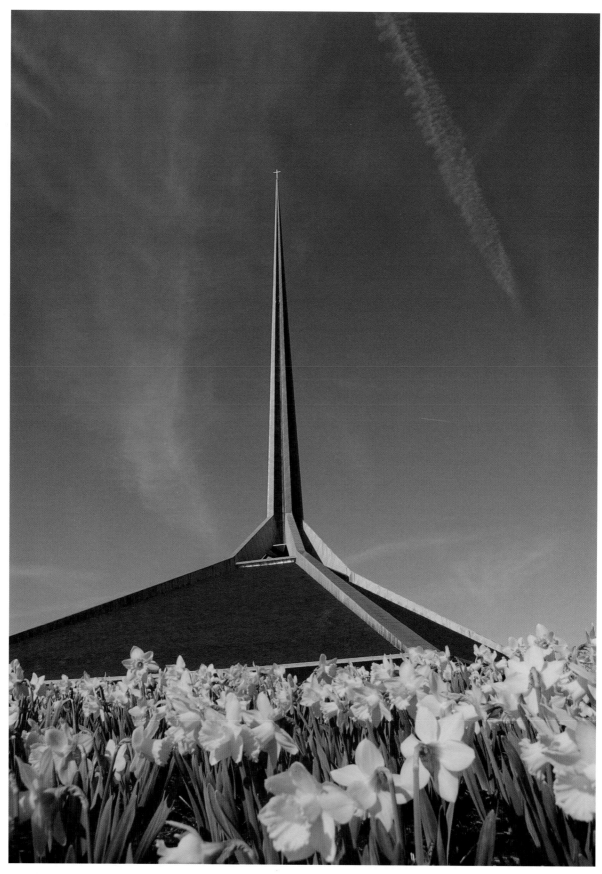

North Christian Church of Columbus in spring. Founded in 1955, it is part of the Christian Church (Disciples of Christ). One of the many notable architectural achievements that has made Columbus famous, North Christian Church was designed by Finnish-American architect Eero Saarinen and completed in 1964. Saarinen said of the church design: "We have finally to solve this church so that it can become a great building. I feel I have this obligation to the congregation, and as an architect, I have that obligation to my profession and my ideals. I want to solve it so that as an architect when I face St. Peter I am able to say that out of the buildings I did during my lifetime, one of the best was this little church, because it has in it a real spirit that speaks forth to all Christians as a witness to their faith." It is the last building the architect designed before the his death in April 1961.

Powers Church, Angola, is a northeastern Indiana historic site on the National Register of Historic Places. The small community of Powers is gone, but visitors can visit the church, which is unchanged since it was built in 1876. The church bells still ring from the bell tower; the 1876 clock still keeps time; and kerosene lamps still light the sanctuary.

Pinhook United Methodist Church near La Porte. The church, built in 1847, was fully restored in 1988.

Luis Cortes portrays Jesus Christ during the annual Good Friday Via Crucis (The Way of the Cross) enactment, sponsored by Our Lady of Guadalupe in East Chicago.

Eli Lilly and Co.

Eli Lilly

Eli Lilly and Co.

J.K. Lilly Sr.

Eli Lilly and Co.

J.K. Lilly Jr.

Ronald J. Waicukauski

The Indianapolis Museum of Art is one of the many institutions in Indiana supported by Lilly Endowment Inc., an Indianapolis-based, private philanthropic foundation created in 1937 by three members of the Lilly family—J.K. Lilly Sr. and sons J.K. Jr. and Eli—through gifts of stock in their pharmaceutical business, Eli Lilly and Co. In keeping with the wishes of the three founders, Lilly Endowment exists to support the causes of religion, education and community development. In creating the Endowment, the founders' foremost priority was to help the people of their city and state build better lives. The Endowment also supports selected causes of national significance, especially in religion and in minority higher education. One of the Endowment's most significant accomplishments in Indiana has been its Giving Indiana Funds for Tomorrow (GIFT) initiative, which has supported the development of community foundations in all 92 Indiana counties, more than any other state. Since its inception and through the end of 2014, Lilly Endowment paid grants totaling $8.5 billion, of which $5.98 billion supported organizations in Indiana.

Bloomington-based Cook Group co-founder Bill Cook and his wife, Gayle, took an interest in historic preservation projects. With generous financial and construction management support from the Cook family, Indiana Landmarks transformed a 19th-century church into Indiana Landmarks Center, a 21st-century cultural and performing arts center and state headquarters for the historic preservation group.

Indiana philanthropy is often individual acts of kindness, small and large.

Friends of McCormick's Creek in Owen County volunteer in the Adopt-A-Highway program.

His Holiness the 14th Dalai Lama has given public talks at the Tibetan Mongolian Buddhist Cultural Center in Bloomington.

Indiana Voices: Eva Mozes Kor

Eva Mozes Kor is a survivor of the Holocaust, a forgiveness advocate, and a public speaker. Born in 1934 in the tiny village of Portz, Romania, her family was sent to the Auschwitz death camp in 1944, where she and her twin sister were subjected to human experimentation under Josef Mengele. After first immigrating to Israel, she married and has lived in Terre Haute since 1960.

"I arrived in Terre Haute 55 years ago—a young bride who did not speak any English. It was a difficult beginning, as all beginnings are. But ultimately, the community accepted me, as well as my children who were born and raised here. Terre Haute became the first real home I had since my family was taken to Auschwitz. CANDLES Holocaust Museum and Education Center has become my way of giving back to Terre Haute, a gesture of my thanks and appreciation.

"I originally founded the museum as a way of remembering my twin sister Miriam. I was trying to cope with my own pain after her death in 1993. She and I survived Auschwitz together, and we were the only ones who survived from our family. Two years after she died, I decided to try an idea: starting a museum in her memory. I didn't have any money and I didn't know how to do it, but the idea was always more important to me than the place. Now that the museum has grown, I see it is a wonderful thing to have a place where young people can look at exhibits and explore the ideas of peace and forgiveness.

"Forgiveness has become the essence of my philosophy of life because it removes the victimhood mentality from a survivor, and it empowers and liberates all victims if they practice it. A world where victims are healed creates a very peaceful atmosphere, and I prefer it over anger and revenge. I hope the community will continue to help spread these simple ideas of remembering, educating and healing for generations to come."

CANDLES Holocaust Museum and Education Center

Young visitors at the CANDLES Holocaust Museum and Education Center in Terre Haute

Members of the Indiana Sikh community work together to provide food for the Midwest Food Bank. Beginning with the arrival of the first Sikhs in Indianapolis in 1967, today there may be more than 5,000 Sikh families in the state, served by nine Sikh temples, called Gurdwaras.
KP Singh

Children in the Jewish Community Center's Big Eagle Camp in 1948. The Indianapolis Jewish Community Center in Indianapolis has been a neighborhood and community resource for 100 years, first at 23rd and Meridian streets and at its current location on Hoover Road on the north side of the city.
JCC Indianapolis

WKVI Radio personalities Tom Berg, Lenny Dessaier and Jerry Curtis at Five Star Grocery Store go live on the air to raise money for Starke County Community Services.
Jim Shilling, Starke County Historical Society

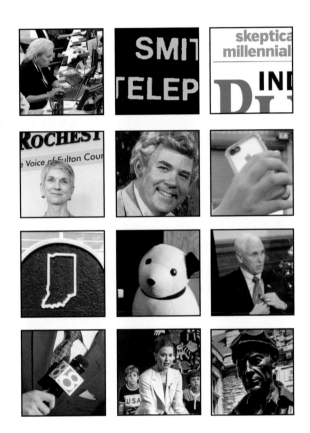

By Eunice Trotter

It was a hot August day in 1976 when I walked into the newsroom of the family-owned Indianapolis Star. It was my first day as a reporter for the state's largest daily newspaper. I could count the number of women in the newsroom on one hand. I saw no other African-American reporters.

The odors of cigarette smoke and coffee were strong. There was the faint aroma of alcohol here and there. The constant ticking sound was wire service machines cranking out breaking news. The pecking noise was from manual typewriters.

This was the traditional newsroom—noisy, white male-dominated, gritty, hardworking, tough and concerned about the communities it covered. This period was the heyday of investigative journalism. The Star had just won a Pulitzer Prize for uncovering police corruption. I was a 23-year-old wanting a Pulitzer of my own.

Media were the watchdogs. Their job was to oversee the decisions and integrity of public officials, provide information readers needed to make daily decisions and advocate for the little guy.

Reporters' tools were the pen and notebook, a tape recorder and typewriter. Television and radio looked to newspapers to determine what they needed to report. Newspapers monitored television to make sure nothing was missed. A political endorsement from The Star could determine who won or lost an election. That was power.

News reaches Indiana consumers in many ways, but like journalists throughout the state, Purdue University English major Elena Sparger still hones her craft in a traditional format as well as through new media.
Purdue University, Mark Simons

continued

Profit margins provided families like The Star's Pulliams with resources they needed for multi-generational wealth. Yet, the paper took care of its people—providing staff with perks like the Fourth Estate, a family outdoors retreat in Lawrence, Indiana; scholarships for their children; and other help. The media business was more than a business. It was family, taking care of its own while also serving the public.

For more than 200 years, media in Indiana have played a critical role in the lives of Hoosiers. The letter, delivered by carriers on horseback or by mail coach, the pamphlet, stump speaking and the telegraph were some of the early communication tools.

Not until Elihu Stout arrived in Vincennes in 1804 to publish the state's first newspaper, the Indiana Gazette (later named the Western Sun), was there mass media in Indiana.

Other early newspapers in the state included Madison's Western Eagle, started in 1813; Corydon's Indiana Herald began in the state's founding year of 1816, the same year as Vevay's Indiana Register and Brookville's Plain Dealer. The Indianapolis News, founded in 1869, would become the state's largest newspaper until The Indianapolis Star surpassed its circulation.

"There's always been technology: the electric typewriter, the word processor, the fax machine. But nothing has allowed such direct and instantaneous communications with masses as the technology of today."

There were also numerous ethnic newspapers in Indiana, including publications appealing to the German, Polish, Jewish and African-American communities. The Indianapolis Freeman, the first illustrated black newspaper in the U.S, was founded in the city in 1888. Das Volksblatt was the first German paper, established by Julius Boetticher in 1848. Spanish-language papers didn't come along until the 1990s.

Radio became accessible to the masses in the early 1920s and listening to it was a family activity. The first radio station was WGAZ radio, now WSBT, which went on air in 1922 in South Bend.

In 1949 Sarkes Tarzian, an ethnic Armenian, started the first television stations in Indiana: WFBM-TV Channel 6 in Indianapolis and WTTV Channel 4 in Bloomington, which became the model for other small-town markets.

WSBT-TV in South Bend became the first television station to broadcast in color in 1954. It is the oldest CBS affiliate in the state. By the 1950s, televisions were in thousands of Hoosier households.

Today in Indiana, there are more than 70 daily newspapers, dozens of weeklies, 40 full-power television stations and 400 AM and FM radio stations.

While Hoosiers continue to value these traditional sources of information, they no longer depend on these media or their news cycles. They access news and information whenever they want it and from a wide variety of sources.

They want it on their cellphones, iPads and laptops. Hoosiers, especially Xers, Ys and Millennials, have enthusiastically welcomed the Digital Age.

What has caused this shift? Technology is the primary driver of the change, say media professionals. There's always been technology: the electric typewriter, the word processor, the fax machine. But nothing has allowed such direct and instantaneous communications with masses as the technology of today.

Throughout the 1980s and 1990s, ownership of many newspapers and television and radio stations shifted from families who lived in the communities they served to out-of-state-based corporations, many of which are publicly held and stockholder-driven.

Such was the case in 1980, when the Northeast Indiana Fort Wayne News-Sentinel, founded by a Hoosier in 1833, was purchased by Knight-Ridder, then by McClatchy Corp. and most recently by West Virginia-based Ogden Newspapers.

The Star and other papers owned by the Pulliam family throughout Indiana and Arizona is another example. In 1998, the $2 billion sale of The Star and its sister papers in Muncie, Richmond and Phoenix to publicly held Gannett Corporation became the largest transfer of media ownership in Indiana history.

After a 16-year absence from The Star, I returned to work there again as an editor in 2002. Gannett now controlled the paper. A woman was now publisher. Another woman was managing editor. Other women and African-Americans, including the black woman editor who recruited me, filled other midlevel and lower management roles. Smoking and drinking were prohibited. Computers were on every desk. Everyone had voicemail. And sometimes you could hear a pin drop.

Journalism had changed. No longer were reporters marching in with their day's news that they uncovered by covering their beats. Instead reporters were sent out to get specific angles for specific stories. No longer did union contracts prevent reporters from taking pictures. Now, it was expected that reporters would not only take pictures, but record video as well. There was a Web desk with three or four staff members whose job was to post to website "chunks" of news for quick consumption by readers. Getting it online fast and first was the goal. These shorts would become longer stories in the next day's newspaper. Convergence, as this combo news coverage is called, was in full swing.

In following years, these strategies did little to stop the plummeting circulation and ad revenue that caused layoffs of reporters, editors and photographers. Small papers were not immune. The Indianapolis Recorder, the 120-year-old black weekly I owned, had a circulation of 50,000 in the 1950s. Today, it has a circulation of less than 5,000. But some small-town Indiana papers like The Corydon Democrat, published since 1856, remain the source of local news for their communities, albeit now on the Web, Facebook and Twitter as well as in print.

Does all this change mean the end of journalism? That's doubtful. Reporters working in this changing newsroom culture are still committed to the principles of journalism. Some free-distribution papers around the country are attracting younger readers. But the jury remains out on what media of the coming decades will be like. Stay tuned.

After a first job as a Teen Talk columnist for The Indianapolis Recorder, Eunice Trotter was the first African-American editor at The Indianapolis Star. She once owned controlling interest of The Recorder and, later, her own public relations business. She now is communications specialist for American Senior Communities.

Smithville Fiber

Workers install the Smithville Telephone Co. corporate logo in the 1960s; today the company is Smithville Fiber, provider of high-speed fiber communications and data. Beginning in the 1920s, telephones linked Hoosiers to each other—and local news—through small companies like Smithville. The nearly century-old company emerged from the pioneering work of Indiana communications legend J.K. Johnston, who connected Monroe County stone quarries with telephone exchanges beginning in 1922. The family ancestors of Darby A. McCarty, today's chairman and CEO of Smithville Fiber, purchased and expanded telephone service throughout areas of southern Indiana and created a nationally recognized company.

Indiana Voices: Sarah O. Wilson

Sarah O. Wilson is owner and publisher of The Rochester Sentinel.

"The Rochester Sentinel is a home-owned daily newspaper whose reason for existence is the same today as when founded in 1858: To reflect life in Rochester and Fulton County as fairly, impartially and objectively as possible.

"The Sentinel's daily task is also to provide support, encouragement and leadership in all matters that will improve the quality of life in our north central Indiana community. During Indiana's bicentennial year, 158 years after The Sentinel's founding, our staff remains proud of our status as an independent daily.

"My late father, Jack K. Overmyer, joined The Sentinel staff when in high school, began full-time work in 1952, later bought the paper and devoted the rest of his life to The Sentinel. My husband Bill and I joined him in 1982, after graduating from Indiana University's School of Journalism and working in the news business in Anchorage, Alaska and Kansas City, Missouri.

"The Sentinel, the oldest continuous business in Fulton County, was there when the city streets were first paved, when the downtown Arlington Hotel burned down and when a tornado ripped through our area. We helped close a toxic landfill and nourish youth sports. Bill embedded with the National Guard in Iraq. We created the Sentinel Scholar awards and Athletes of the Week for our three area schools.

"We launched our website in 1997 and have added videos, an electronic edition and a mobile app. We post to Facebook and tweet. Our best days are when our subscribers tell us how The Sentinel can help make our community even better."

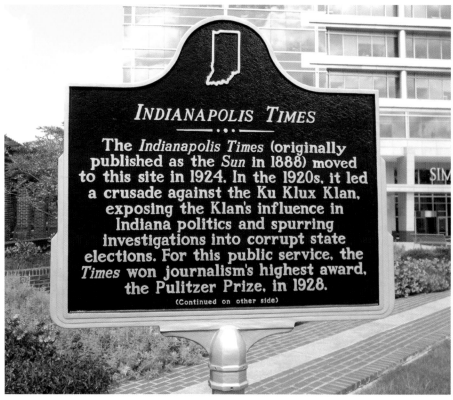

Indiana Historical Bureau

News media in Indiana report history and, sometimes, make history.

RCA in Indiana began with the production of radio tubes in Indianapolis in 1930. In 1954, the first commercially successful color TV came off the RCA—Bloomington assembly line. By 1956 plants in Monticello, Marion, Indianapolis and Bloomington encompassed the largest TV production concern in the world. During the early 1970s, RCA employed nearly 30,000 Hoosiers and RCA's Consumer Electronics sector remained headquartered in Carmel as a division of Thomson until 2007.

The Children's Museum of Indianapolis

On June 1, 1979, local TV station WTHR became an NBC affiliate. To mark the occasion Indianapolis native and Today Show cohost Jane Pauley broadcast part of the popular morning program live from The Children's Museum.

WTHR-TV

WTHR-TV weatherman Bob Gregory interviews Indianapolis native and Broad Ripple High School graduate David Letterman following the announcement that Letterman would host "The Late Night Show." The show premiered in 1982; Letterman stepped down as host in 2015.

Indiana Voices: Leah Johnson

Leah Johnson is a 2015 journalism graduate of Indiana University, where she was digital editor of the Indiana Daily Student and where Pulitzer Prize winner Ernie Pyle served as editor-in-chief in 1922.

"Ernie Pyle's legacy is the lifeblood that courses through every story, every beat, and every paper that we [at the Indiana Daily Student] publish. Ernie managed to cut through the pretense of war and celebrity to deliver something fundamentally human in his columns. He gave us a first-hand look at the unexpected beauty and ever-present tragedies of the frontlines. And that day, as I read his words, the last he would ever write, I remembered those things. I was overwhelmed with the magnitude of it all; what journalism is, the purpose it serves and the lives it can touch long after we're gone. Ernie Pyle taught us—and continues to teach us—that the key to storytelling is unabashed truth. Above and against all else, Pyle's work stands as a reminder to us all that we tell stories for the ones who can't."

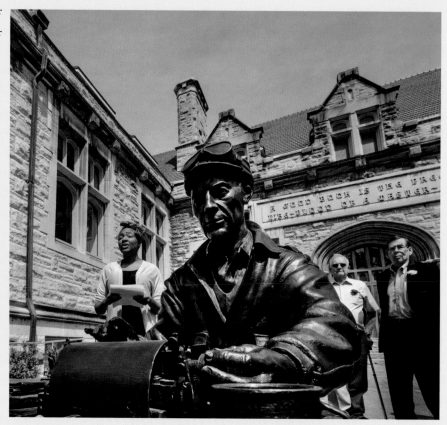

Steve Raymer, Indiana University Board of Trustees/The Media School

Student Leah Johnson reads Pyle's last column during the commemoration at Indiana University in Bloomington of the 70th anniversary of Pyle's death.

Indiana State Library Collection

Ernie Pyle in 1940. His birthplace in Dana is now the Ernie Pyle World War II Museum.

Reporter Bennett Haeberle and videographer Jason Harris of WISH-TV in Indianapolis cover a trial in Tippecanoe County.

Shawn Pierce

Students at work in Ball State University's Unified Media Lab.

Michael Hickey, Ball State University

Taking a selfie at the Indiana State Fair. A 2014 Pew Research study found that half of social network users have shared news stories, images or videos and nearly as many have discussed a news issue or event. An increasing number are creating their own news by posting photos or videos of news events.

John Whalen

Indiana Voices: John Krull

John Krull is director of the Pulliam School of Journalism at Franklin College.

"When Indiana entered its first century as a state, news was both expensive and hard to come by. Newspapers were rare, frequently supported by government contracts and often passed around rural communities like treasured heirlooms.

"Now, as Indiana begins its third century as a state, much has changed. News is everywhere—in print, on the air, on the screen of the computer the average Hoosier owns and even in the cell phone he or she carries almost everywhere.

"This very abundance of news—and the myriad ways businesses now have to communicate with their customers—battered the business model

TheStatehouseFile.com

As a Franklin College senior in 2014, Jacob Rund interviewed Indiana Gov. Mike Pence for TheStatehouseFile.com, a multimedia news site powered by Franklin College journalism students.

that sustained journalism in Indiana and elsewhere for more than a century. Now that advertisers don't need newspapers, TV newscasts and radio stations quite as much they once did, those so-called legacy media have struggled to adapt.

"The stresses on the old business model for news operations have often diverted attention from the opportunities journalists now have to work more closely with their audiences.

"New, more collaborative and, in many ways, more efficient models have sprung up. Most newspapers, TV news programs and radio newscasts have become more collaborative and interactive. Many new not-for-profit news operations—Franklin College's TheStatehouseFile.com and Chalkbeat Indiana, for example—that combine partnerships with legacy news organizations and strong support from targeted and motivated audiences have sprung up.

"A single theme runs through these changed or new operations—a redefined relationship between journalists and their audiences. The old communications model in which journalists wrote or spoke and the audience read, watched or listened is disappearing. Replacing it is a new model that has journalists and their audience sharing news and responses more immediately and more constantly.

"Once upon a time we journalists called that a marketplace of ideas.

"What once was old now is new again."

INFact

The Society of Professional Journalists, the nation's most broad-based journalism organization, was founded on the DePauw University campus (as Sigma Delta Chi) in 1909. DePauw is also home to the first 10-watt college FM radio station in the country, WGRE-FM, which went on the air in 1949. DePauw's student-managed and award-winning newspaper, The DePauw, is the oldest college newspaper in Indiana.

Indianapolis Business Journal debuted in 1980 as a weekly publication devoted to local business news. One of the first local business newspapers in the country, IBJ has won numerous national awards and now has a robust online news presence to complement its print product.

Indiana High School Press Association

The Daily Echo (Sept. 26, 1898). In 1898, Shortridge High School in Indianapolis established a daily newspaper, The Daily Echo. It was the first daily high-school newspaper in the entire country, and was edited by Kurt Vonnegut Jr. when he was a student there. Although it became a weekly in the 1970s and ceased publication with the school's closure in 1981, Shortridge re-opened as a Magnet High School in 2009 and students brought back the Echo as well.

Indianapolis Star employees work at the Digital Hub at the center of the newsroom in new office space in Circle Centre mall. The Star moved in September 2014 from its 107-year-old building to the mall, backfilling some of the space that once housed a Nordstrom department store.

The Indianapolis Star

FABLES in SLANG By GEORGE ADE · Stone Chicago

THE HOOSIERS · NICHOLSON · THE MACMILLAN COMPANY

A CHRISTMAS STORY · JEAN SHEPHERD

JOHN GREEN · looking for alas

BREAKFAST OF CHAMPIONS · Kurt Vonnegut, Jr.

BEN HUR · WALLACE · HARPERS

The Magnificent Ambersons · TARKINGTON · SAGAMORE PRESS · S-2

Stratton-Porter · Freckles · THE LIBRARY OF

WEST · THE FRIENDLY PERSUASION

Dan Wakefield · UNDER THE APPLE TREE · DELACORTE PRESS · LAWRENCE

AN OLD SWEET HEART OF MINE · JAMES WHITCOMB RILEY · BOWEN MERRILL

By Susan Neville

Indiana is landlocked. You must pass through several states or one state and one province to reach an ocean. The state would have been as perfectly rectangular as Colorado and Wyoming if it weren't for two bodies of water: Lake Michigan and the Ohio River. And so the familiar shape of Indiana: a box turning into lace on the south as though a romantic surveyor, while laying out the borders, began with a piece of string and attached it taut across the northern and eastern boundaries and then later in the day stopped to gaze at the Ohio and the Wabash. And so the string was allowed a bit of fancywork until the surveyor remembered, around Vincennes, that this was to be a straight-laced state.

Both art and culture in Indiana have always contained that tension between the fixed line and the fluid. When I talk about the fluid, think of the large inland sea that once covered this ground, of the swamps and rivers and the dense hardwood forests. Think of wildness as opposed to domesticity, of freedom as opposed to restraint. When I talk about the fixed, think of township lines, straight rows of corn and soybeans and fences and canals and interstates and railroad tracks. A grid.

In the great Indiana novel of the 20th century, "Raintree County," Ross Lockridge Jr. writes that "the formal map ... had been laid down like a mask on something formless, warm, recumbent, convolved with rivers, undulous with flowering hills, blurred with motion, green with life. He mused upon this mingling of man's linear dream with the curved earth, couched in mystery like a sphinx."

continued

The works of famous Indiana authors, past and present, grace the shelves of the Indiana State Library. A sampling, from top to bottom: George Ade, Meredith Nicholson, Jean Shepherd, John Green, Kurt Vonnegut Jr., Lew Wallace, Booth Tarkington, Gene Stratton-Porter, Jessamyn West, Dan Wakefield, James Whitcomb Riley.

John Whalen

Indiana Voices: Anila Quayyum Agha

Artist Anila Quayyum Agha, an associate professor of drawing at Herron School of Art and Design, won both the popular and juried grand awards in the 2015 international ArtPrize competition for her installation "Intersections"—the first time in the competition's history that a single artist won the top awards in both categories. Agha was inspired by a 2011 visit to the Alhambra palace in Granada, Spain, made possible by a New Frontiers travel grant from Indiana University. She is also a 2009 recipient of the Efroymson Contemporary Art Fellowship. A native of Pakistan, Agha has made her home in Indianapolis since 2008.

Herron School of Art and Design

"I work in a cross-disciplinary fashion with mixed media, creating artwork that explores global politics, cultural multiplicity, mass media, and social and gender roles in our current cultural and global scenario.

"Living and working in Indianapolis has been good for me. The faculty and staff at Herron School of Art and Design at Indiana University welcomed me. Becoming a part of the larger community within Indianapolis and the state allowed me to contribute in meaningful ways through teaching and working within the arts community.

"Participating in the rejuvenation of Indianapolis has been really wonderful. I believe the arts and humanities have made great contributions to the cultural and economic boom that is apparent in Indianapolis. Over the last eight years I have noticed there is greater appreciation of the contributions of Indiana artists, as well as opportunities for cross-cultural dialogue among organizations doing wonderful work and benefiting our society across divides."

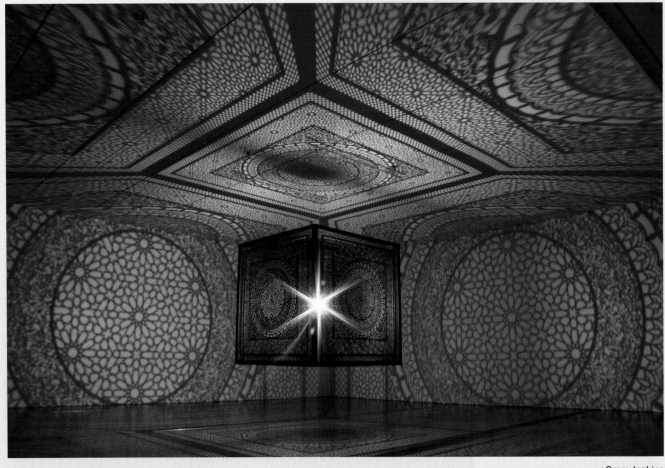

Gram Jenkins

"Intersections" by Anila Quayyum Agha

Author Kurt Vonnegut keeps his eye on his hometown of Indianapolis in this mural by artist Pamela Bliss, "My Affair with Kurt Vonnegut." The Kurt Vonnegut Memorial Library, which opened in 2011, honors his memory with a collection of his books and drawings, along with exhibits and educational programs.

Authors James Whitcomb Riley and Meredith Nicholson with Hewitt Hanson Howland, the editor who worked with them at Indianapolis' Bobbs-Merrill Publishing Company (undated).

"I often speak of appreciation, both of nature and art, as the art of seeing beautifully."

~T.C. Steele

In this 1921 painting by Indiana artist Wayman Adams. Hoosier Group artists T.C. Steele, Otto Stark, J. Ottis Adams and William Forsyth appear to be watching a current-day visitor to the Indianapolis Museum of Art. The Hoosier Group of impressionist artists, which also included Richard Gruelle, attended art school together in Germany. Works by the Hoosier Group are represented in a number of Indiana museums, including the Ball State University Museum of Art, Indiana University Art Museum, Richmond Art Museum, Swope Art Museum in Terre Haute and the Indiana State Museum.

Indiana Voices: Donna Weaver

Donna Weaver, a wax-sculpture artist living in Vevay, has the unique distinction of having her initials carved on a U.S. quarter. She designed and sculpted the Indiana state quarter, one of many state quarter designs she created for the United States Mint's 50 State Quarters Program. She also sculpted the design for the U.S. circulating nickel. Today, Weaver sculpts miniature wax portraits of historical figures, including Indiana's William Henry Harrison, George Rogers Clark and the early-19th-century author and teacher Julia Dumont.

"I was creating wax portraits long before I started working for the U.S. Mint. My late husband and I were doing living history enactments, and I was looking for things that were interesting to me. At the time I worked for Kenner Toys, sculpting toys in wax. While waiting for somebody at a library one day I grabbed a book and saw the wax miniatures. I said, 'Bingo! I can do that.'

"For me, the joy of sculpting is the doing of it. It was a pleasure to be able to sculpt the Indiana quarter. It took about a week to create. My initials are on it, in the southeastern corner of the state, where my house is.

"I live in an 1836 house that sits on the Ohio River in Vevay. I'm also a volunteer at a National Historic Register site, the Musee de Venoge, in Switzerland County's wine region. The history is so rich and varied in this section of the state, especially being on the river, which was the highway early on. All that wonderful history is one of the things I like about southern Indiana. It's got it all here."

Weaver designed and sculpted this medal commemorating the 2013 bicentennial of the town of Vevay.

Weaver's portrait of early Indiana author and teacher Julia Dumont.

Quilting is an art form popular in Indiana since the pioneer days. The Barn Quilt Trail in Marshall County features quilt-patterned murals on barns and buildings, while the Quilters Hall of Fame museum in Grant County preserves the National Historic Landmark home of Marion native Marie Webster, one of the most influential quilt designers of the early 20th century. This design was created by quilters in Daviess and Warrick Counties.

The Haan Mansion Museum of Indiana Art features a large collection of Indiana art. Originally the State of Connecticut building at the 1904 St. Louis World's Fair, the mansion was dismantled and moved to Lafayette, where it became a private residence and now is also a museum.

Indiana cartoonist Jim Davis created the popular lasagna-eating cat "Garfield," who greets visitors at many spots along the Garfield Trail in Grant County, where Davis grew up. This photo shows the "Paws for Thought Garfield" in Marion. Davis's studio is located in Delaware County.

Samara, a 1956 West Lafayette house designed by famed architect Frank Lloyd Wright, is a National Historic Landmark. Also known as the John and Catherine Christian House, it is one of the most complete Frank Lloyd Wright homes in the U.S., having been occupied only by its original owners since construction.

Indiana Voices: Bob Jacobsen

Starr-Gennett Foundation

Trumpeter Bix Beiderbecke and his band recorded at Gennett Records in Richmond in the 1920s.

Bob Jacobsen is secretary of the board of the Starr-Gennett Foundation in Richmond, which educates students about Indiana's jazz heritage and one of its most famous record companies, Gennett Records.

"'Stardust,' one of the most beloved and recorded songs, was written and recorded in Indiana. Hoosier songwriter Hoagy Carmichael recorded 'Stardust' at Gennett Studios, a division of the Starr Piano Company that operated in Richmond from 1872 to 1952. Others who recorded at Gennett include Louis Armstrong, Joe 'King' Oliver, Jelly Roll Morton, Bix Beiderbecke, Gene Autry, Lawrence Welk and Guy Lombardo.

"Today, the Starr-Gennett Foundation is helping students learn about the music and musicians of Gennett Records. The Gennett Records Walk of Fame is in Richmond."

Starr-Gennett Foundation

Local schoolchildren learn about jazz through the work of the Starr-Gennett Foundation.

During the first half of the 20th century, Indiana Avenue in Indianapolis was a breeding ground for many nationally recognized jazz musicians, including Wes Montgomery, Dr. David Baker, Freddie Hubbard, J.J. Johnson and Slide Hampton. The Duke Hampton Family Orchestra is shown here in an undated photo, with Slide Hampton playing the trombone.

Duncan Schiedt Collection, Indiana Historical Society

Sullivan Fortner, the 2015 recipient of the American Pianists Association Cole Porter Fellowship in Jazz, performs with the Buselli Wallarab Jazz Orchestra at the finals of the 2015 competition at the Hilbert Circle Theatre. The national contest is held every four years in Indianapolis.

Mark Sheldon

International Violin Competition of Indianapolis Gold Medalist Jinjoo Cho and pianist Rohan De Silva perform during the ninth quadrennial competition at the Scottish Rite Cathedral in 2014. The contest, founded in 1982 by Indiana University Jacobs School of Music teacher and violinist Josef Gingold, showcases the world's best young violinists.

Denis Ryan Kelly Jr.

Indiana Voices: Simmie Williams

John Whalen

Graphic designer Simmie Williams grew up in Gary, around the corner from the family who went on to earn international fame as the Jackson Five. He still keeps in touch with Jackson Five family members today and has designed graphics for their projects and, most recently, their "Unity" tour. He's shown here standing in front of the Jackson family home in Gary and its shrine to pop superstar Michael Jackson, which attracts visitors from around the world.

"Growing up in Gary during the 1970s allowed me to see The Jackson Five as more than just a musical act. Their hard work and dedication clearly demonstrated how such commitment to one's craft can truly pay off and take you to the very top.

"This is still a valid lesson for our youth in Gary today and into the future."

René Stanley, Indiana Bicentennial Commission

This tribute to Hoosier rocker John Mellencamp is on display at the Jackson County Visitor Center in his hometown of Seymour.

Courtney DeRusha

Indiana singer-songwriter Jennie DeVoe performs at the Blues at the Crossroads Festival in Terre Haute.

206

Shawn Spence

The Eiteljorg Museum of American Indians and Western Art in Indianapolis is the only museum of its kind in the Midwest, and one of only two museums east of the Mississippi that explore both Native America and the American West. Its collection of contemporary Native art is ranked among the world's best.

Brown County Convention and Visitors Bureau

The Bill Monroe Music Park and Campground in Bean Blossom is home to the oldest continuously presented bluegrass festival in the world.

Ball State University

"The Circus in Winter" was created in 2010 by students and faculty at Ball State University as an adaptation of English professor Cathy Day's novel of the same name. It follows the lives of an Indiana circus owner and the cast of talent he hires. It was staged at the university before making its national debut in 2014 at Goodspeed Musicals, the two-time Tony Award-winning theater in Connecticut.

Built in 1924, The Lerner movie and concert theater in Elkhart was restored in 2011. It now offers a year-round calendar of theater, dance, music and other entertainment options.

Dance Kaleidoscope, Indiana's oldest professional contemporary dance company, has been performing since 1972. The company performs its season concerts at the Indiana Repertory Theatre in Indianapolis and tours throughout the state and nation.

The Fountain Park Chautauqua in Remington, built in the 1890s, is one of only three chautauquas in the U.S. in continuous operation since their establishment. Developed in the late 1800s, these summer assemblies feature educational, religious, entertainment and cultural programs.

The grave of movie star James Dean is routinely adorned with tributes during the four-day Remembering James Dean Festival in Fairmount, held every September in the town in which he spent much of his youth.

The Indianapolis Symphony Orchestra, founded in 1930, continues to be one of the nation's most renowned orchestras. In 2011 Krzysztof Urbański began his tenure as the seventh music director of the ISO—the youngest music director of any major American orchestra at the time.

The La Porte City Band, one of the oldest in the United States, sits for a photograph in 1911. Today, the band performs free summer concerts at La Porte's Fox Park.
La Porte County Historical Society

The monthly jazz jam session at Paul Henry's Art Gallery in Hammond
Thomas Semesky

Live theater in Indiana runs the gamut from professional equity companies to small community theatres. Cardinal Stage Company, shown here, is a professional theater company in Bloomington. It presented Neil Simon's "Brighton Beach Memoirs" during its 2014-15 season.
Blue Line Media Productions

INFact

A Few Filmed-in-Indiana Movies

Breaking Away (1979) – Bloomington
Brian's Song (1971) – Rensselaer
Eight Men Out (1988) - Indianapolis
A Girl Named Sooner (1975) – Vevay
Going All the Way (1997) - Indianapolis
Hoosiers (1986) – various locations
Indianapolis Speedway – Indianapolis (1939)
A League of Their Own (1992) – Evansville
Rudy (1993) – Notre Dame, South Bend, Whiting
Some Came Running (1958) – Madison
Speedway (1929) – Indianapolis Motor Speedway
Winning (1969) – Indianapolis Motor Speedway

David Blase

David Blase (standing, right), the real-life inspiration for the movie "Breaking Away," accepts the Little 500 trophy in May 1962 for his winning Phi Kappa Psi team. Kneeling at bottom left is another team member, Steve Tesich, who wrote the screenplay for the 1979 movie. Blase, who pedaled 138 of the 200 laps in the Little 500, sometimes sang Italian opera while he cycled—just like the character portrayed by Dennis Christopher in the film. Blase grew up in Speedway while Tesich hailed from East Chicago, Indiana.

Harmon Photography Inc.

Every July, the Peru Amateur Circus presents performances featuring 200 young people between the ages of 7 and 21. The event, sponsored by Circus City Festival Inc., honors Peru's circus heritage. Many of the country's famous circuses wintered in Miami County beginning in the 1890s, and the area is now home to the International Circus Hall of Fame.

Rona Schwarz

The Simon Skjodt International Orangutan Center at the Indianapolis Zoo is the home of eight orangutans, including Katy, pictured here. The center has one of the largest groups of these Great Apes of any U.S. zoo.

210

Founded in 1925, The Children's Museum of Indianapolis is the largest children's museum in the world. Its collection of 120,000 artifacts and specimens, along with 11 major galleries and permanent and special exhibitions, attracts 1.2 million visitors each year.

This pen-and-ink illustration by Indianapolis artist KP Singh highlights the state's historic courthouses. Born in India, Singh came to the United States in 1965.

By Bob Hammel

Indiana had not yet celebrated its first centennial when 1911, its most momentous sports year, came along.

We were ninth-largest in our 46-state nation then, with two more seats in the newly apportioned House of Representatives than California, and midway through a period of 60 years when the U.S center of population was in Indiana. In 1911, that center was a spot just outside a furniture factory in downtown Bloomington, walking distance from where something enduring began. An Indiana University students' Boosters Club struck gold with an idea: recognize the new sport of basketball by inviting the best high-school teams in Indiana's 13 congressional districts to IU for a state-championship tournament. Twelve came and history began.

On March 11, 1911—just 20 years after the game was "invented"— Crawfordsville defeated Lebanon, 24-17, for Indiana's first high school basketball championship. "Hoosier Hysteria"—what the entire nation now knows as "March Madness"—was born, a quarter-century before the first NCAA tournament.

continued

Sarah E. Carlson

Basketball, particularly the high-school version, fit burgeoning Indiana perfectly. Towns and townships proudly supported their high schools, many of them small, so basketball was the perfect school sport: only five players were needed to field a team. In 1912, the Indiana High School Athletic Association ran the tournament, limited to boys until 1976. It kept the finals in Bloomington but opened participation to all IHSAA members. By 1915, 385 teams were playing in newly designated "sectionals" that picked the 14 who came to IU for 13 games in two days. Tiny Thorntown was crowned champion that year.

In 1928, Butler University's astonishing new 15,000-seat fieldhouse wooed a tournament that now had 740 teams. That building was Hoosierland's Mecca in the tournament's richest years—through The Depression into the post-war '40s to 1971, constantly introducing some of the sport's grandest names. Johnny Wooden, later an All-American at Purdue and a coaching nonpareil at UCLA, starred for Martinsville in the first championship game at "The Fieldhouse," heartbroken that night by a last-minute, center-court shot that won for Muncie, 13-12. Everything peaked when little Milan's run to the 1954 championship (the Cinderella story that inspired the classic 1986 sports movie "Hoosiers") was followed in 1955 by Oscar Robertson leading Indianapolis' all-African-American Crispus Attucks team to the nation's first integrated state championship. Attucks also won in 1956, becoming the first undefeated Indiana champion.

"The State"—two semifinal games on a March Saturday afternoon, the championship game that night—for more than 50 years played to constant sellouts. On March 25, 1990, the epic popularity of a folk hero named Damon Bailey—featured on Sports Illustrated's cover as an eighth-grade wunderkind—moved the tourney on its final day to the spacious Indianapolis Hoosier Dome, a football building. There, a national high-school record crowd of 41,046 watched senior Bailey score his Bedford North Lawrence team's last 11 points for a comeback 63-60 championship-game victory over Concord. He graduated as the state's all-time leading scorer. He still is.

Those two 1911 staples, basketball and the Indy 500, continue as symbols of sports in Indiana.

Indiana basketball wasn't the only great tradition born in 1911. About 80 days after the first "State," Ray Harroun left racing retirement to win the first Indianapolis 500-mile auto race—in a self-designed, Indianapolis-built Marmon "Wasp." The Memorial Day race quickly became the international identification of Indianapolis and auto racing.

Along the way it survived a mid-1940s crisis. Unused during World War II, the Speedway track had grass poking through its racing surface when Terre Haute businessman Tony Hulman injected a post-war charge of money and imagination that swelled "500" crowds to upwards of 400,000—unmatched by any sports event anywhere. The event's aura faded some when Dixie-based "NASCAR"—the "SC" standing for stock car—passed Indy's sleek racers in national fan following. But even NASCAR's biggest names—e.g., Jeff Gordon, who first raced as a 14-year-old on Indiana tracks—jumped at the chance to race at Indy in 1994 when the Indianapolis Motor Speedway introduced the annual Brickyard 400.

Those two 1911 staples, basketball and the Indy 500, continue as symbols of sports in Indiana. With some notable company.

This is, after all, the state of Notre Dame football: Knute Rockne, The Gipper, The Four Horsemen, the Golden Dome—does sport get bigger than that? And, overshadowed as they are by the Irish, Purdue (with a quarterback tradition from Cecil Isbell in the '30s through Bob Griese in the '60s to Drew Brees in 2000) and Indiana have had football All-Americans and bowl teams, too.

Indiana's baseball heritage also runs deep. The sport's first pro game was played on May 4, 1871, at Fort Wayne: the hometown Kekiongas vs. Cleveland's Forest City. Ancient Hall of Famers "Three-Fingers" Brown (Nyesville), Amos Rusie (Mooresville) and Edd Roush (Oakland City) preceded Chuck Klein (Fort Wayne) and Max Carey (Terre Haute), followed in national renown by Carl Erskine (Anderson) and Gil Hodges (Petersburg) of the Jackie Robinson Dodgers, World Series "perfect game" pitcher Don Larsen (Michigan City), and more recent All-Stars Don Mattingly (Evansville) and Scott Rolen (Jasper). The game's modern-day savior, "Tommy John Surgery," began on a Terre Haute-raised arm. When Cooperstown opened its Hall to pre-Robinson stars of the Negro Leagues, homegrown Oscar Charleston of the Indianapolis ABCs went in.

Indianapolis is in America's big leagues with its 2006 Super Bowl champion Colts, basketball Pacers, and a strategy of hosting national and international sports championships to boost the economy. Perhaps the city's crowning achievement was Super Bowl XLVI in 2012.

Today, IU proudly flies five collegiate national-championship basketball banners, while Purdue and Notre Dame, Butler, and in flashy moments Indiana State, Ball State, Evansville and Valparaiso all have had their own highlights—e.g., an all-timer of the sport, Larry Bird, ISU '79.

More recently, women have seized equality in opportunity to make their own headlines, particularly in basketball with NCAA-championship teams at Purdue (1999) and Notre Dame (2001) and a professional championship for the Indiana Fever. Those, and the state high school tournament that began for Hoosier girls in 1976 and has sent dozens on to college and pro careers, came after an opportunity-equality mandate that itself was Hoosier-based: "Title IX," the 1971 Education Act, authored by Indiana Sen. Birch Bayh Jr.

Hoosiers pioneered other equal opportunities in athletics, too. Shelbyville's Bill Garrett broke the "gentlemen's agreement" that had kept African-Americans from playing basketball at Big Ten schools when he joined Indiana University's team in 1947. A year later, IU's George Taliaferro become the first black player drafted by the National Football League.

Did longtime IU men's soccer coach Jerry Yeagley have a crystal ball when he elevated the sport to varsity status in 1973? He started IU on a course to win eight national titles by 2015 in a sport whose popularity is soaring today in an increasingly diverse Indiana. Youth soccer leagues pack Hoosier playgrounds. The 2014 World Cup drew thousands to a culture-blending, outdoor game-watching party in downtown Indianapolis. The professional Indy Eleven premiered the same year, selling out every game. Even cricket is on the horizon, with teams across the state.

But our calling card remains basketball, our hearts beat fastest when the green flag drops at Indy, and our golden year is 1911. Hoosiers of extraordinary vision ennobled us forever then. Their modern-day counterparts might even be in our midst today.

Bob Hammel was a sports columnist in Bloomington for more than 40 years and is a member of the U.S. Basketball Writers Hall of Fame.

The Special Olympics Indiana Summer Games showcase the awe-inspiring abilities of athletes with intellectual disabilities.
Lesley Ackman

Former Indiana University football star George Taliaferro was the first African-American drafted by an NFL team.

Coach Joe Tiller and quarterback Drew Brees led Purdue to the 2001 Rose Bowl. Brees, who went on to a successful NFL career, was the latest in a long line of quarterback greats from Purdue, often referred to as the "Cradle of Quarterbacks."

Notre Dame football is one of the most iconic programs in the history of collegiate sports.

A fall tradition: the annual Monon Bell Classic. The small-college football rivalry between DePauw University and Wabash College began in 1890.
Richard Fields

Indianapolis hosted Super Bowl XLVI in 2012, the culmination of more than three decades of using sports to draw visitors and economic activity to the city.
Mike Briner

The Indianapolis Colts defeat the Seattle Seahawks 34-28 at Lucas Oil Stadium in Indianapolis. The Colts arrived in Indianapolis in 1984 and won the Super Bowl in 2006.
Aaron P. Bernstein, Indianapolis Business Journal

Indiana Voices: Allen Miller

James Miller

Allen Miller, age 97, had never played or coached basketball, then world events intervened. At the school where he taught history, the basketball coach was abruptly drafted to fight in World War II, and, as Miller says, "the principal drafted me to coach." The team he inherited midseason won the 1942 county championship. By the next school year he was teaching and coaching in Indiana, at Jefferson Township School in Elkhart County. Miller's story of how he was hired for his next job and what happened later illustrates the importance of the game in Indiana.

"Harold Watson was the Washington Township Trustee in Elkhart County. At that time the trustee was responsible for the local schools, including the hiring and firing of teachers and coaches. He hired me away from Jefferson Township to coach at Bristol, a rival school. At Jefferson I had no six-foot players. Bristol was loaded with big guys. We beat Bristol with careful defense, causing Mr. Watson to exclaim, 'That don't go.' That's when he hired me to take over at Bristol.

Allen Miller

Bristol High School's 1946 team, coached by Allen Miller, center of front row.

"Watson and the coach I replaced both had sons who were excellent players, and they were both on my team. Rifts developed between the fathers, and it was not long before their ongoing feud was obvious on the basketball court. I knew that I had to nip this in the bud. At what I considered the appropriate time I called both of them to my 'office' in the basement. My comments were brief. 'I love you both, you are great players, and I need you, but the community knows about your dads and it shows on the floor. This has got to change. You two will either get along or both of you are gone.'

"The upshot was they shook hands and promised to put feelings aside for basketball. The result is that these two helped take us to the final game in the sectional tourney at Elkhart."

The 1954 Indiana state champions from Milan inspired the movie "Hoosiers" and have their own museum in the Ripley County town.
Katherine J. Taul

Indianapolis Business Journal

George Hill starred at Broad Ripple High School and IUPUI before playing for the Indiana Pacers of the NBA. The team started in 1967 in the old American Basketball Association, where it won three championships. After the ABA folded, the Pacers joined the NBA, where they reached the Finals in 2000.

Camille Dunne, Butler University

Butler University's Hinkle Fieldhouse was the largest basketball arena in the United States when it opened in 1928. It retained that title until 1950.

Brent Smith, Butler University

Butler University basketball fans didn't have to go far to cheer on their basketball team in the 2010 NCAA Championship game. The Bulldogs played perennial power Duke University at Lucas Oil Stadium in Indianapolis, which hosted seven Final Fours between 1980 and 2015, more than any other city.

"In the end, it's about the teaching, and what I always loved about coaching was the practices. Not the games, not the tournaments, not the alumni stuff. But teaching the players during practice was what coaching was all about to me."

~ John Wooden

John Wooden starred in basketball for Martinsville High School and Purdue. He then coached in high school and at what was then Indiana State Teachers College on his way to an unheard of 10 national championships as coach of UCLA.

The Indianapolis Star

Indiana Voices: Bill Hampton

In 1955, Crispus Attucks became the first Indianapolis team to win the Indiana high school basketball championship and the nation's first all-black team to win a state championship. But because of attitudes about race that prevailed at the time, Attucks' team wasn't treated to the traditional victory lap around Monument Circle. That honor was bestowed 60 years later, when members of the team were honored as grand marshals of the 2015 500 Festival Parade. Bill Hampton, a guard on the championship team, talks about the significance of the championship and how times have changed.

"It was a big deal to win the state championship back then because that was our goal, but I didn't realize the magnitude of what it would mean. You don't think about it every day, but when it's been 60 years, it brings back a lot of memories.

"Racism was rampant then, but the powers that be who determined what happened at that time are gone, and people today are determined to right that wrong. The recognition we are getting, well, it's humbling and you just appreciate what you have right now. The 500 Festival Parade was fantastic. It was mind-boggling, because it was just a sea of people. They were just as happy as we were. They showed us so much love and appreciation.

"When you see how people react now, you wonder how [the racism] ever happened. It's a big transformation."

John Whalen

Bill Hampton (right) with former Attucks teammate John Gipson.

Indiana Historical Society

Crispus Attucks' 1955 high school championship team

The Purdue women's basketball team brought a national championship home to West Lafayette in 1999.
Purdue Athletics Communications

Indiana University

Quinn Buckner, left, and Scott May celebrate after Indiana defeated the University of Michigan for the 1976 NCAA championship. The '76 Hoosiers remain the last Division I NCAA basketball team to complete the season and tournament without a loss.

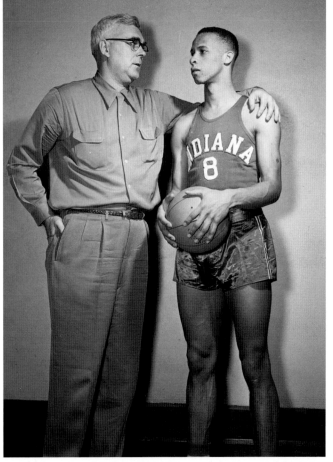

Indiana University

Bill Garrett of Shelbyville was the first African-American to play on the IU basketball team and also the first to regularly start on a Big Ten team, opening the league to full integration. The 1951 All-American is shown here with Coach Branch McCracken.

Many high-school gyms throughout Indiana are filled to capacity for Friday and Saturday night basketball games. Here, Floyd Central High School cheerleaders urge spectators to show their team spirit.
Julie Kaiser

Indiana Voices: Emmeline Seest

Gail Baker Seest

Emmeline Seest, 10, plays youth soccer in Rossville, in Clinton County. Below she tells why soccer is her favorite sport.

"1.) I love soccer and know many people who haven't ever played soccer before. I know that they are missing out on an awesome sport.

"2.) Soccer helps people have better eye-foot co-ordination. It teaches kids to work with other team-mates and get along better. Also, kids who play soccer will (usually) have good sportsmanship.

"3.) Soccer means a great deal to me. I've played with my share of good players and bad players, but I still believe that soccer is one of the best sports, and I know other people who play soccer would agree.

"4.) I think that it would be pretty awesome if, on the World Cup, people hear this on the loud-speaker: ''that goal was scored by none other than (insert name here) from Indiana!!!"

The IU men's soccer team celebrates after winning its eighth national title in 2012.

IU Athletics

Indianapolis Business Journal

The Indy Eleven, a team in the North American Soccer League, started play in 2014. Its supporters, who call themselves the Brickyard Battalion, predate the team. They organized in 2011 with the goal of bringing professional soccer to Indianapolis.

The Indianapolis Star

Soccer's growing popularity in Indianapolis was evident in 2014 when fans gathered on Massachusetts Avenue for an outdoor viewing party to watch the U.S. team in World Cup play.

Indiana Voices: Marco Andretti

Marco Andretti is a third-generation IndyCar driver, following in the footsteps of his grandfather, 1969 Indianapolis 500 Champion Mario Andretti, and his father, Michael Andretti:

Andretti Autosport

"Everyone says that it's just another race, but it isn't—it's THE race. Indianapolis is our Mecca; it's the big one. We work our whole careers for the chance to say 'I'm an Indy 500 Champion.' I grew up around racetracks, but coming to Indy every year is what stood out the most. My fondest memories are sitting at the old Brickyard hotel and hearing my father and grandfather's names over the PA. 'It's a new track record!'—the words we waited for each day. As a family, so far we only have one win at Indy, but I think we've been blessed. We've had a ton of podiums, a ton of runner-up finishes as a family and we're not done. Another win here would mean the world."

Ralph M. Reed

The Indianapolis Motor Speedway infield has been a draw for race fans, like these fans in 1941, since the first Indy 500 in 1911.

The Indianapolis Motor Speedway's traditional Victory Lane was upgraded in 1994 with this circular rotating lift.

Denise Lundy

Indiana University's Little 500 bicycle race was started in 1951 to raise money for student scholarships. It was the subject of the Academy Award-winning movie "Breaking Away" in 1979.

Marshall "Major" Taylor was a Hoosier cyclist who overcame racial discrimination to win national and world cycling championships. His first European race, shown above, was held in Berlin. He won 47 of 54 races in Europe that season.

Marc Marquez, a Spanish grand prix motorcycle racer, takes part in the Red Bull Indy Grand Prix, one of several events now held at the Indianapolis Motor Speedway, once reserved only for the Indianapolis 500. NASCAR's Brickyard 400 is also a fixture at the track.

The Marian University cycling team has earned 29 national championships since its inception in 1992.

IN Fact

Ten Hoosiers in the Hall

These 10 Hoosier-born baseball players represent Indiana in the National Baseball Hall of Fame:

Mordecai Brown
Inducted: 1949
Primary team: Chicago Cubs
Primary position: pitcher
Hometown: Nyesville

Max Carey
Inducted: 1961
Primary team: Pittsburgh Pirates
Primary position: center fielder
Hometown: Terre Haute

Oscar Charleston
Inducted: 1961
Primary team: Pittsburgh Crawfords
Primary position: first baseman
Hometown: Indianapolis

Ford Frick
Inducted: 1970
Primary position: MLB Commissioner
Hometown: Wawaka

Billy Herman
Inducted: 1975
Primary team: Chicago Cubs
Primary position: second baseman
Hometown: New Albany

Chuck Klein
Inducted: 1980
Primary team: Philadelphia Phillies
Primary position: right fielder
Hometown: Indianapolis

Sam Rice
Inducted: 1963
Primary team: Washington Senators
Primary position: right fielder
Hometown: Morocco

Edd Roush
Inducted: 1962
Primary team: Cincinnati Reds
Primary position: center fielder
Hometown: Oakland City

Amos Rusie
Inducted: 1977
Primary team: New York Giants
Primary position: pitcher
Hometown: Mooresville

BASEBALL
Hall of Fame

Sam Thompson
Inducted: 1974
Primary team: Philadelphia Phillies
Primary position: right fielder
Hometown: Danville

226

Evansville Otters

Built in 1915, Bosse Field in Evansville is the third-oldest ballpark still in regular use in the United States, surpassed only by Fenway Park (1912) in Boston and Wrigley Field (1914) in Chicago. It is home to the Evansville Otters and was used to film "A League of Their Own."

La Porte County Historical Society

La Porte native Charles O. Finley owned the Oakland Athletics Major League Baseball Team, which won the World Series in 1972, 1973 and 1974.

Victor W. Pleak

The Indianapolis Indians play at Victory Field, carrying on a proud tradition of baseball in Indiana.

> *"The skiing center of the world is southeastern Indiana, where I like to call home. It looks like the Alps there; it's crazy."*
>
> *~ Nick Goepper*

John Whalen

Dearborn County's Nick Goepper with his bronze medal for free-style skiing at the 2014 Olympics in Sochi, Russia.

Indiana State Fair Commission

The Indy Fuel of the East Coast Hockey League brought professional hockey back to Indianapolis.

Jim Young, Indianapolis News

Indiana University swimming phenomenon Mark Spitz won an unprecedented seven gold medals at the 1972 Olympic Games in Munich.

Steve Blackwell

Rodeo events like calf roping, shown here in Boone County, help fill out a diverse sports calendar in Indiana.

227

The Eagle Creek Reservoir rowing course in Indianapolis was the first internationally certified course in the United States and has hosted among many competitions the 1994 World Rowing Championships and the 2005 U.S. Rowing Championships, shown above. Rowing is among the many sports Indianapolis used to stake its claim as an amateur sports capital capable of hosting national and world championships.

Ball State women's volleyball coach Steve Shondell took over the program in 2010 after leading the Burris Laboratory School in Muncie to an impressive 1,183-95 record over the course of 34 years. Under his guidance, the Burris Owls won 21 state championships, four national championships and finished with undefeated records seven times.

The Tamika Fever Drum Song

Tamika Catchings, 2012 MVP
2012 Indiana Fever, WNBA Title
2015 Inductee, Indiana Basketball Hall of Fame
2015 Sports Humanitarian of the Year

Four ten minute quarters, halftime,
sometimes overtime, five players on two teams,
coaches, the bench and the ball
which flies to the net from wherever
she stands. Tamika, three syllables, Olympic
gold medalist, Catchings, her name.

Just as a poem has rhythm, she passes the ball
and in an exact, exquisite assist, it soars
out the fieldhouse door,
down the street and into our lives.
In a matchup with the stars,
inside-out and beyond the arc, she rules.

Feel the beat to compete
and Tamika records quintuple-double
digits: 25 points, 18 rebounds, 10 steals,
11 assists, 10 blocks. In the third stanza,
dribble to the end of the line and shoot.
Are you watching? She steals the "**b**".

In the first line of the fourth stanza,
her ball bursts into alphabet.
On and off the court,
she knows where shout comes from—
the fever drum sounds, no one like her,
daughter, shot clock girl, Catchings, listening.

~ Elizabeth Krajeck

Indianapolis Business Journal
Tamika Catchings, one of the most prolific players in the WNBA, led the Indiana Fever to the league championship in 2012. She's also a mentor to young athletes, especially at-risk youth.

By Sandy Eisenberg Sasso

This chapter is dedicated to all of our children, the ones of whom Hoosier poet, James Whitcomb Riley, wrote:

> To all the little children: — The happy ones; and sad ones;
> The sober and the silent ones; the boisterous and glad ones;
> The good ones — Yes, the good ones, too; and all the lovely
> bad ones.

The prophet taught, "Your old shall dream dreams and your youth shall see visions." (Joel 3:1)

Looking back is like dreaming. As in our night imaginings, we relive what frightened us, delighted us, troubled us and what made us proud. Our dreams refashion what was in ways that are necessary to ground us and to help us move on. Our dreams tell our stories; they edit our past so that we can go forward.

But visions are something else. They look beyond past and present and see something that has not been, but yet can be.

Our young people in Indiana see visions. They imagine more green spaces, parks and bike paths; less violence, racism and religious prejudice; better education, and public transportation. They want an outdoors where it is safe for them to play, explore and wander.

Their visions may make you smile; they may also surprise you. Children told me that they want less social media. We might be amazed to learn that adolescents are exhausted from the constant public exposure of their every act. Teenagers want to be able to whisper without broadcasting every word to the public. They yearn for privacy and to be able to keep a secret.

continued

Exploring the indoor playground at The Commons in downtown Columbus.
Ronald J. Waicukauski

They decry bullying, talk of websites that are mean, intrusive and hurtful. They love their cell phones, yet complain of too many electronics. They say, "Go outside." In a world where most people seem plugged into something, they yearn for more quiet. One young person said, "Listen. Ask us what is best for us. We know something." They want a future where they have our undivided attention and our uninterrupted listening.

Students worry about exclusion and favoritism, stress and anxiety. They feel that everyone is in a hurry and want to slow down. They are afraid that others will be too "intractable" to change their views. They are afraid that they might be as well. They envision stronger communities and neighborhoods where there can be debate without yelling and conversation without judgment.

"It is easy to forget that delightful promise and spontaneity of youth. Every so often we should visit the world of children, so we won't forget."

Our youth freely express their gender identity, and they hope for more openness to others who are different. A young 18-year-old, born in Darfur, came to Indiana when she was 3 years old. She talks about the negative comments she receives when wearing her hijab. Her vision, which reflects the vision of so many others of her age, is for greater diversity and a more cosmopolitan Indiana. High school students express the hope that when people visit this state, they will feel accepted and welcome with open arms. They abhor narrow-mindedness. They celebrate change and understanding.

A high school student of Chilean and Syrian ancestry imagines a future filled with challenges. She says, "I never want to stop and ask myself 'Is this all there is?' I think of life as a current, and I plan on riding the current."

No matter where their families are on the economic ladder, every child wants to be successful, to have an education, a house, a job, a family. Those who grow up in poorer neighborhoods have those same dreams, but when asked of what they are afraid, they say, "of getting killed; of dying." They are 14 years old. Students at the Indiana School for the Blind worry about guns and safety. Our youth remind us of those things for which we will be held accountable in the next century: inadequate education, poverty, hunger and homelessness, pollution, violence and intolerance.

Our young people are annoyed by the provincial and parochial stereotypes they have heard about Indiana. They do not see themselves that way. Most do not want Indiana to be considered a "flyover" state. They do not want to be put down. As one ninth-grader remarked, "We have people with dreams, talents and brains." They imagine a state with more excitement, life and energy, a place with a soul, even as they find simple pleasure in saying that what they really like about Indiana is that it's home.

They dream big and want to make a difference. And they do. A sampling of some of the young people who have won the Indianapolis Children's Museum's Power of Children awards offers a glimpse of the grand ideas the next generation has for the future. They see a problem not as a crisis, but as an opportunity.

From providing computer access to seniors and underserved communities to supporting U.S. troops, from creating Rolling Libraries 4 Kids to providing affordable electric wheelchairs, our children have the passion and the dedication to change the community. A young cancer patient who created Tatum's Bags of Fun for newly diagnosed children reminds us, "Children should realize that they can do anything they put their minds to."

Optimism and idealism are marks of childhood. As we age, our visions are often tarnished. It is easy to forget that delightful promise and spontaneity of youth. Every so often we should visit the world of children, so we won't forget.

The trunk of the Constitution Elm in Corydon, under which the Indiana Constitution was partly written in 1816, still stands. If we nurture the imagination our children see, their visions will grow from that trunk and flourish, providing shade for future generations.

Indiana has traveled from mammoths to monuments, from Ku Klux Klan to cultural trail, from insularity to greater inclusivity. Throughout our state we have places to remember Indiana as it was and is. The voices of our children help us imagine Indiana as it can be. In their words, "Be open, be wild and be enthusiastic about life." "Become the epitome of what America stands for: justice, freedom and equality."

From the banks of the Wabash to the star atop the flame of the torch of liberty, from the limestone quarries to the fields of corn, from the cheers for our sport teams to the applause for our symphony and theater, from the halls of our museums to the classrooms and laboratories of our schools and universities, from business offices to factory floors, may the third century see us proud to call Indiana our home.

Taking part in Indiana Humanities' ALL-IN Block Party at Vincennes University's Jasper campus

Author Sandy Eisenberg Sasso is senior rabbi emerita at Congregational Beth-El Zedeck in Indianapolis and director of the Religion, Spirituality and the Arts Initiative at Butler University and Christian Theological Seminary. The children quoted in her essay are students in Evansville, Elkhart, Indianapolis, Martinsville and Carmel, as well as Children's Museum of Indianapolis Power of Children award winners from throughout Indiana.

Walking with teddy bear near Bloomfield

Watching the sunset in Starke County

Indiana Department of Natural Resources

Whiling away the lazy days of summer at Shakamak State Park

John Kofodimos

Spending time with a kitten in Hendricks County

Joe Heredia

Posing for a summer snapshot on Main Street in East Chicago

Carl Gay

Watching a plane fly overhead

Jackie Sutton

Exploring the wonders of nature on the farm

Indiana State Fair Commission

Learning how to grow vegetables at the Indiana State Fair

Daniel A. Baker

Commemorating the 50th anniversary of the March on Selma in Fort Wayne

Susan M. Dunn

Singing holiday carols at a Johnson County mall

235

Tobogganing at Pokagon State Park in Angola

Tubing at Perfect North Slopes in Lawrenceburg

Strolling in the country

Ice skating at the Indiana State Fairgrounds

Working and playing on a Spencer farm

Dreaming of the lake amid the fields

Riding the roller coaster at Indiana Beach

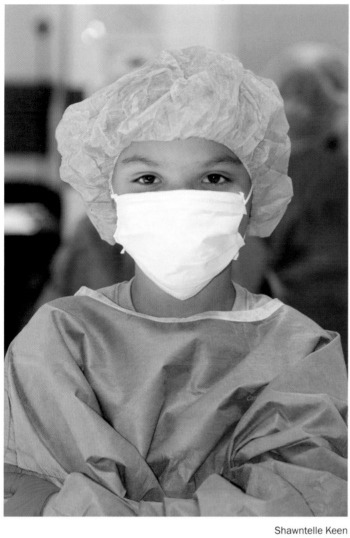

Exploring a potential career

Enjoying a performance in Mishawaka

Transplant

Indiana summertime: a backdrop of cicadas' buzz
as my brother and I race down the Mooresville hill to the path between
our grandparents' fish ponds. My grandmother, hearing us argue—

which one of us started too soon, who pushed who
so they tripped on a sycamore root—

would straighten up from rows of pea tendrils and trailing cucumber vines
where she was pulling thistle and chickweed. She'd raise an arm to her brow
half to shade her eyes from the relentless sun, half to say

cut it out, you two. Always summertime, with tin pie plates clanging
in the persimmon trees to scare the crows, and nets strung

over the blueberry bushes. The tails of my grandfather's worn shirt flapping
at her side. She'd dress up—they both would—
for my late August birthday. I'd hear the car doors slam

in our driveway, the call for my mother to come on out and help
carry all these flats of tomatoes. Tucked atop a bushel of new potatoes

would be a gift-wrapped bell pepper, or a jar of homemade pickles
with an old Christmas bow stuck on the lid. I suspect my father
considered it shabby, maybe thoughtless that they hadn't bought me something

precious, likely hadn't even remembered it was my birthday until
my mother's dinner invitation, but how those smooth peppers felt

in my palm, how the flesh would crunch to reveal
some small amount of bitterness like a truth from which my parents would
rather have sheltered me. Like when a snake was startled out from under

the zucchini vines in her garden and my grandmother brought the hoe down
to sever its head, flung the body onto the compost heap, then kept hoeing as if

it were not even a distraction. That might never have happened
but I remember it vividly. I'm alongside her where I'd help sometimes,
weeding in the garden's dusty rows. "You can't leave

any roots," my grandmother would chastise me. What remains
of those summers now that I am gone east and she is gone to ash?

Where I live, a north wind brings the smack of saltwater brine
to every season. When I kiss my own children goodnight
they smell of the sea.

~ Christine Montross

Index

A

B

C

Robert N. Anderson

"Sandhill Sunset"

Rebecca James

"Under the Covered Bridge," Ceylon/Geneva

242

I

J

K

"Northern Cardinal"
Matt Williams

"Queens at Dawn," Arcadia

Sally Meyer Wolf

Rhonda L. Mullen

"The Sunset Curl," Lake Michigan at Portage River

Harvest in Cass County

Judi Barr

Jessica Bussert

"Fog House," Brown County

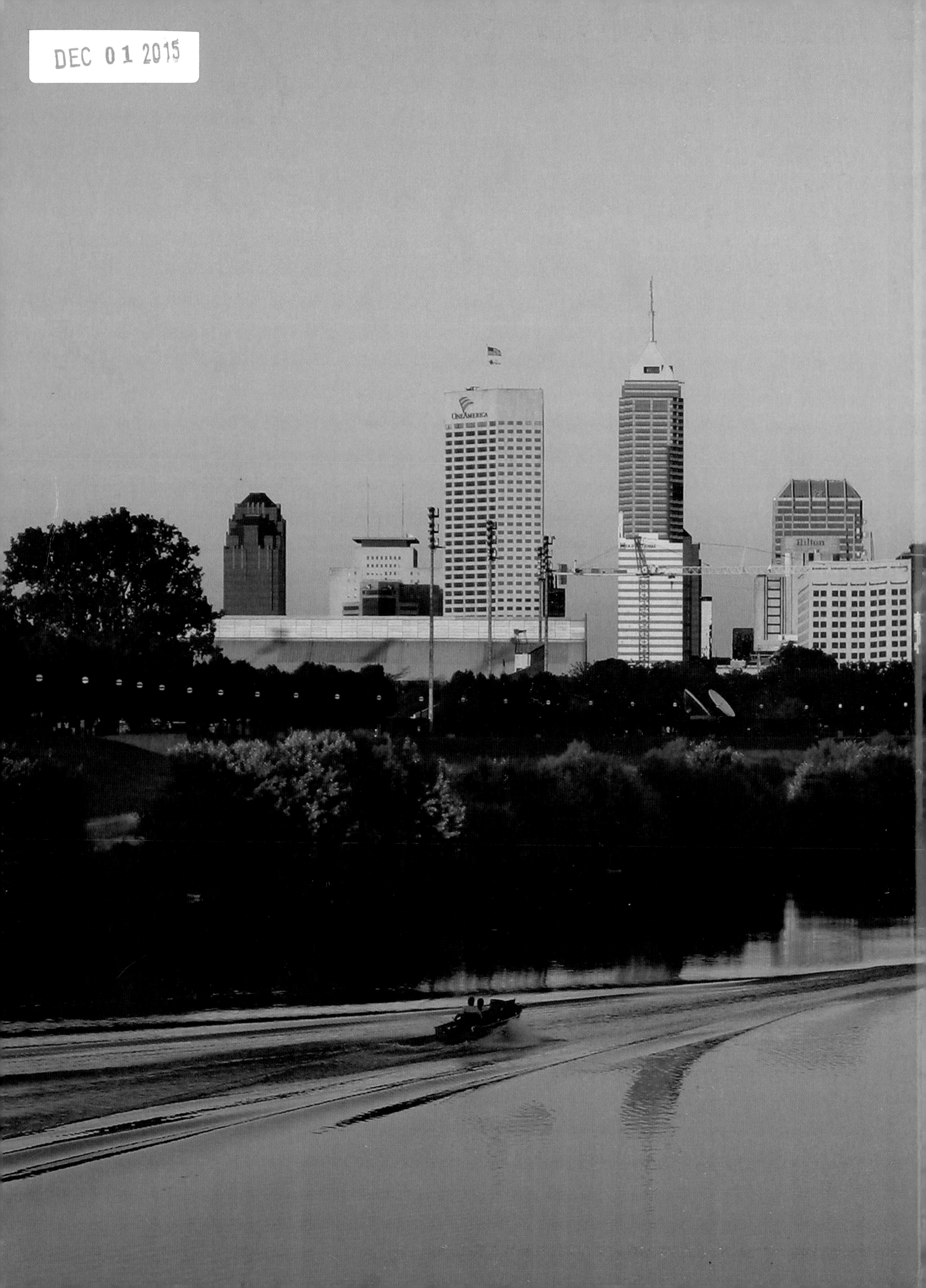
OneAmerica
Hilton